Unexpected Harvest ~ A Gathering of Blessings

edited by
Ruth Moon Kempher

illustrations by
Wayne Hogan

Kings Estate Press, 2005
St. Augustine, Florida

- ACKNOWLEDGEMENTS -

Due to space constraints, indexing and the listing of prior publications are included with the Contributors' Notes at the back of the book.

Our special thanks to Michael Hathaway and Chiron Review Press, for typesetting and other help.

ISBN: 1-888832-20-7

Published by
KINGS ESTATE PRESS
870 Kings Estate Road
St. Augustine, FL 32086-5033
rmkkep@bellsouth.net

This collection is dedicated, gratefully, to those good small press editors of the past, the present, and with hope, the future, who labor often without thanks, to keep the craft alive.

WINDOWS

that open like wounds filled with
light

Duane Ackerson

CHILDFOOT VISITATION

One night traveling a Green Tortoise bus
    San Francisco to Seattle,
The rear of the bus converted to pads for sleeping,
Sleeping on my back as we plunged through pouring rain,
    the other weary passengers sleeping,
Suddenly something moving in my beard and under my nose
    woke me up –
Opening my eyes in the darkness
    I saw in the flickering headlight patterns
    of passing cars
The small foot of the little girl sleeping
    beside her mother.
Cleansmelling childfoot flower stretching beneath my nose
    as she changed position in her dream.
Gently pushing it away, careful not to wake her,
    I drifted off to sleep
Thinking how many men who never had a child
    are visited by a childhood foot
    slowly sliding through their beards
    opening their eyes to
    its perfect shape in the twilight?
Suddenly out of Eternity coming to me
    white and pink and smelling good,
For the first time in my life
    a little girl's naked foot
    woke me up.

Antler

PULLING THE CAUTION LIGHT

The moment when
something shifts –
not in a perverse way,
not a dropping out
from under you
like a crazy
California earthquake,
but the kind
of movement
a conductor would
cause, raising
his magician's wand
over the band,
everything suspended;
a traffic light, a
warning signal on
a movie set, the buzzer
going off in your
kitchen, something
about to begin, a taste
you can hardly wait
to eat. Pulling the
caution light
out of existence.

Ann Menebroker

TANGLES

Morning. My daughter scolds
   the hairbrush and
      the tangles and me,
because I pull and thread:
   puzzle the knots,
      mending night's thrash and dream
with my two hands, daily.

Through the screen door,
   sounds of Asia:
      bamboo chimes clack
in disarray:
   storm tumbled them
      into a twisted grove.
In Java, in Bali, wind through
   bamboo is a common sound –
      villagers untangle and
mend the weave daily.

Life is a fishnet.
   I make of my hours
      a constant undoing –
unsnarl the playground from
   my daughter's curls,
      untie the shoe, unhook the burrs.
So I untwist the bleached strings
   of bamboo chimes; I need
      their memories of Asia, soft gossip,
mild talk about the weather, daily.

I need uncommon sounds:
   I will pull and thread
      and mend, again.

I will find a gold carp
   in my daughter's hair,
      a glade of bamboo
by my teacup,
   an island in the backyard
      created with my
two hands, daily.

Ann E. Michael

EIGHT YEARS OLD

Even in winter, my son refuses to wear
a pajama top. When he comes near,
I lean close and brush his skin
or stroke it outright
like bolts of wedding satin,
and something catches in my throat
like undissolved chocolate
in a cup of cocoa. He is lush,
toes pink and curled
as the pearly hearts of seashells,
voice lifting and plunging,
a heron diving for fish,
his pogo-stick stride,
arms like clock hands gone wild,
the balloons of his cheeks when he grins,
and on his restless legs, faint hairs
pointing in all directions
as if ruffled by wind,
a great storm on the way.

Terry Godbey

LITTLE BROTHER

1.

Butterflies don't hurt you.
No, I said.
Bees hurt you.
Only if you bother them, I said.
Wapses hurt you.
Yes.
Butterflies don't hurt you.
No.
I wish I were a butterfly.
Why, I asked.
So I wouldn't hurt anyone.

2.

When you toss somebody into the sea
say you're sorry
take him out again
save him
and bring him home with you
and never hurt him again.

If you hurt him again,
I'll call the police!

3.

There are two gods –
the sun and the moon

Carolyn Sobel

GRANDMOTHERING

Upon reading Hansel and Gretel
for the umpteen-hundredth time;
first to siblings, then my children
and, now, my grandchildren;
I am amazed to find I am still
in this story.

No longer the brave sister
trying to save her little brother,
nor, the concerned parent;
I have become the wicked grandmother witch
trying to force the little ones
into the oven of conformity.

Dorothy Jenks

BECOME AS A CHILD

Each year, I look back and find that my most memorable Christmases all occurred about 35 years ago. Our youngest daughter, who is now 5'7" and sleekly athletic, was then a stocky, round child with white-blond angel's hair. And every year, for at least four years, there was a round, blond cherub beneath our Christmas tree, arms outstretched for her next present.

"Oh! It's *yust* what I always wanted!" our cherub would shriek. And then she would open her present.

Margaret Shauers

ARTS & SCIENCES

Latin verbs were the first to change
Her coltish heart. The sweet demands
Amo amas amat, which led to other verbs
Wakened her to certain rhythms as surely
As the softball did her eyebrow when she was ten,
Turning away, as the first tightening of the tether
Of geometry did for her crazy bone.

And now, the physics teacher announces
Everything we used to count on its tentative,
The sun itself adrift in a universe
That may or may not have started out of nothing.
The clockmaker on the faculty says the pendulum
Might just as well swing up and away,
And when we are all set for the steady rush
Homeward, might throw us skyward for a lark.

He says the coming down may be too quick,
That this certain world, this globe, may jolt
To a halt, one of those carnival bumper cars
When the juice is cut. The only time he grins
Is when he dismisses the steady pull of gravity
As no more absolute than a lover's sigh
Smack in the middle of a kiss. His voice reminds her
Of an altar boy's, pretending to be growly
As a bear's but soft as underwear inside.

Martin Galvin

ON THE OCCASION OF MY DAUGHTER'S 40TH BIRTHDAY

You were the first, so both sets of grandparents clustered
in a hospital waiting room thought it was after two a.m.
First grandchild and first girl since the birth of your mother.
What a beautiful child, perfect in every part.
Your gowned father wheeled you out of the delivery room
showing you off, calmed, cleaned of birth fluids, swaddled
in pink, sleeping off your birth trip.
You turned my life upside down.
Why didn't anyone tell me: you will never be the same.
Nothing like this will ever happen again with quite the same
intensity, wonder, newness. With this child you'll have time –
if you're lucky – to connect the dots.
With this blessing you're thrown into worlds
you never suspected.

Laurel Speer

EIGHT MONTHS

Hakim, Hakim,
your mother is thirteen.
Your granma says you crawl
like you got roller skates for knees,
When I press close
to listen to your heart
over your shoulder I still see
the sunbeat vacant lot.
Quiet, calm, wise,
you let me look into your ears.
Your hand is on my cheek.
I've known your family
fourteen years.

Kelley Jean White MD

HOW THE THING LATEISHA SAYS SHOWS SHE HAS MORE SENSE – LATEISHA, THE KID FROM THE REAL-LIFE STREET OF THE ALTERNATIVE SCHOOL – MORE COMMON SENSE THAN ALL THE MEMBERS OF THE NEW YORK STATE BOARD OF REGENTS

After listening to instructional material for her essay,
and then, after listening ten minutes to the Listening Passage,
ten minutes of single-spaced-tightly-fonted-
professorially-prepared-pedagogical
boring
blather
about the value of, and tactics to utilize for,
taking notes in the margins of school-assigned novels

> O! The underlying surety of Underlining!
> Hey, ho! The highroad of Highlighting!
> Astonishing! The qualities
> of an Asterisk! Stellar
> Starring!

and other useful pragmatisms
useful to use in Real Life

Lateisha says, getting ready to listen to the Listening Passage AGAIN

I gotta listen again
to ten more minutes
of
this
shit?

Frank Van Zant

HAVE YOU SEEN HER

Has she been here today, have you seen her?
Ask the hooky children, the autumn children
fox-stepping across the vacant lots.
They may have seen her foot print in the frost.
Ask the bad children, they know her.
They know her ragged chrysanthemum hair
and her wild-fire eyes.

Surely she went through the town this morning.
Only a few frowsy birds are left in the tossing trees
and the wind smells persimmon.
Ask the keepers of the little shops, they know her.
Ask Miss Huggins, busy with pencils and candy.
Peppermint, wintergreen, horehound.
Miss Huggins knows her.
All the mongrel dogs run wildly in circles
yipping at nothing.

There are rumors of her in the farmsteads.
Ask the Parson, he knows her, he knows.
Furtive and unrepentant they are
in his october parish
small swirls of laughter behind the hymnals.
The ditches are criss-crossed with cat-ice.
At night an owl hoots from the pine near the belfry.
Parson knows she has been here.
All the bad children run past him
with lanterns in their eyes.

Evelyn Thorne

GREEN BAN

There is so much green
in my consciousness
I do not wear it
or want it
in my house

it is bliss
it taunts me

Tricia Cherin

CHILDHOOD SCENES

everyone has that moment
when a room becomes remembrance
curtains, river view and fragrant breeze
come into focus

"Run, faster, Sis!"

cookie crumbs nestle in old chairs
softness of family lingers
and provides strength
for fateful sled one winter's day

girl stretches arms to spring's wild sky
runs her heart out
dreams of flying
with wind and clouds

sees eclipse of the moon
from bank of trees
with Missouri fog rising

moon reappears
lights river
like a burning scythe
that two-steps over high prairie
around soft-needled pines preening for birds

Marie Asner

ALIVE

There has to be more
than an empty house
holding up the sky,
wind chimes whispering
at the window,
a candle flame licking the quiet.

Say *bell, garland, peppermint.*
Open yourself to the rush of years,
regret tugging at fear's lock.

Pleasure is simple, really.
Step into the hush, the stars
sparking, and drink the dark.
You will swell with hunger,
ready to fatten yourself on love,
do anything for it.

Even the moon,
which has seen everything,
will lean closer
when at last you let the shawl slip
from night's shoulders.

Terry Godbey

NIGHT

Night. How can one word ever begin to describe the beauties and mysteries of that enchanted time from dusk to dawn?

Night is not to be feared. It is to be loved as it folds you softly in its star-encrusted blackness. How absolutely charming if you are lucky enough to be out on a night of regal beauty when the moon is full and clouds are swept about the sky by the soft wind in ever-changing patterns.

Or – to be cozily in looking out as the clouds take complete possession of the sky and are torn only by the jagged pieces of lightning.

Jane Hathaway

IDEALS

At night there is the distance
between the black St. Johns River
and the stars who do not move
as long as I am watching.

All that intrudes
is the foolish owl.

The savage, savage owl
ghosts over his dark
to reign and ride his lady
on rails across the bridge.

William E. Taylor

SAVE AS AN IDEA

Looking up at the stars
    through bodies of microorganisms
        swimming on my eyes,
Looking through translucent protozoans
    who don't know the ocean they swim in
        is my eyes
    or that my eyes can see
        and that there are stars above
    they're looking up at,
        distant suns,
    or that I'm alive
        and can walk, talk, blink, think –
Microscopic unicellular beings swimming
    on the ever-present
        liquid outer-eyeball curve
    I can't see
        but know they're there
    because I read about them
        and saw photos of them –
Tiny, teensy alive-as-much-as-me-beings
    making love on my eyes
        while my eyes take in
    ultimate Milky Ways
        unaware of them
            save as an idea,
        save as knowing they're there
      knowing they're see-through-able to the stars,
Save as feeling if they don't know of me or the stars
    what do I not know of
        that's looking
    through me
    at something far grander
than itself,

Standing on the frozen surface of Devil's Lake
Between looming silhouettes of ancient bluffs
Looking through transparent single-celled beings
        swimming on my eyeballs' surface
                admiring Orion's naked stars
        and the beckoning Pleiades
While fish below snow-covered ice
        don't know of microorganisms on my eyes
                or that I'm above them
        or that the stars are above me
                or that above the stars above the stars
        on another planet in another galaxy
An astronomer looking at our galaxy
        through his telescope thinks
                it looks like an amoeba.

Antler

A LANDSCAPE WITHOUT PEOPLE IN IT

Has no scale so you pose me as a yardstick again.
Don't. I'd rather think this bracken-strewn
slope the size of my thumb, and the sheep
that nibble its windy sky as small as the knots
on the dotted swiss that crossed my bed
when I was a child. That white. That infinite.

Lola Haskins

OCEAN REUNION

Bea & Bruce take Antler & me
to a beach where we find
like Maggie & Milly & Molly & May:
tidepools full of live starfish,
sea urchins, rockfish camouflaged
against underwater rock,
hermit crabs in their borrowed shells.
Bruce gently loosens an urchin
with his pocketknife from the rock
to which it's affixed, places it gently
spines-down on my palm
so its mouthbeak stares at me
from the center of gyrating
red-purple spines.

> Ah Echinoderm
> Weary of Time,
> I hold you
> all in all
> in my hand,
> Little Flower!
> Lilac in the Dooryard
> of Another World.

This *is* another planet.
Snails, seaweed, limpets
are this planet's inhabitants.
And I am an astronaut from outerspace
zooming in on innerspace,
on my knees on an edge
of honey-combed rock terrain
peering into a small tidal pool
somewhere in the Universe.

Jeff Poniewaz

THE OUTER RIM [for Slim Zaremba]

Out there the closest buses are comets.
Inhuman distances devour everything
save our projected eyebeams.

As we peer into the void, we scatter
names and wreckage as a form of homage.
For all our linguistic juggling, Slim,
our world weighs less
than the slightest solar whim.

Still, these baubles keep their balance,
spin and run and bend their grooves
around the rim.

Held at bay, chaos tips its brim
and glances back at the time
before zero, before the blast.

These days, this tiny system
seems well-run, but as you know,
such things can't last.

Out beyond the ruby planet, past
Saturn's necklace, beyond even that
Pantagruel of planets, Jupiter
(a planet so empty, it's only gas), past
the weakened fingers of old Sol's pull,
where even Kupier's Belt belongs
to another, beyond where
Charon strains at Pluto's tether,
Time's weather seems far less cruel.

Blair Ewing

FIELDS

High in the ferngreen sky
daisies grow
infinite, turn petal wheels
in myriad, slow
revolution

while below

in umber fields, the stars
endlessly white, fling splinters

going where galaxies go.

Ruth Moon Kempher

THE SEA

The young woman
stands before the sea
facing to the right with
a camera pressed
against her eyes. The
sea is a molten green spilling
onto the sand. There is
blue to a sky harboring
hoverings of at least
50 opinions struggling
in mid-air.

Wayne Hogan

green night
punta de mita 9/02

silent lightning
green night

(as in the underside of moss)
through salt-stung eyelids

bashed by loco moths
& thick dew air

now bearing flotsam
come great white-lipped waves

to consume their innards
vastly

& with abandon
for all that blocks their way

only now
& after all this

the delayed roll of thunder
applause of wonder

mesmerizing mother of all waters
i join you here

Spiel

I swim near creek bottom
with a school of golden dace
We swim among elodea and vallisneria
the water is cool
all of sky is present in that golden sand
all of life is present in those striped dace
and in the green creekweeds

A large mussel crawls creekedge
a kin snail explores dead wet leaves
I see my life in these workings

A green hummingbird drinks nectar
from a cardinal flower next to the mud path
high vines creak in tops of trees
sun sings down leaves and needles

My wasted world remembers

Will Inman

SUN DANCERS

Two sparks of sight, these mites,
two dancers I'd never see in shade,
did their pirouettes, adagios,
showing off for each other what
they had and why they were fit
to carry on the crafty race
of virtuosos from which they came.
They had a sense, these two,
a way to court with elegance,
that made me wonder how they measure time.
As I watched they flung and flew a life and death,
a way of saying that exceeded words, a physics
without translation. They swirled and ducked
and dived intent only on the other and position,
those dots of is. Their energy put hummingbirds
to school to learn appetite,
their ritual, a complication of space and time,
would make a bishop seem a monk,
their will to be, their grace and need
confounding to the human eye
that had for a minute something true to see,
and then, as it will, the sun went west
and left me with this gift, this loss.

Martin Galvin

THE IRONWEED THAT WILL NOT FADE ...

Caught in a quirk of chemistry I can't explain? Like jellies in primeval swamp that over eons lock into bold mineral forms we're only vaguely conscious we're connected to, yet sense in sudden flashes, risen from some blood-depth below thought, we *are* ... For eight years now the color of that flower's oddly set, as if embracing vision beyond doubt. Violet-purple clusters springing from each upturned flowerhead, as though just plucked upon an August woodwalk when my wife and I had journeyed to the South from Illinois. A summer long ago, our natures yet unformed – when jokingly I'd placed it there (a homely "Druid ritual" to honor our new life?) beneath the hillside window in a terra cotta vase. Criss-crossed, as the years wore on, with spiderwebs upon the bare oak floor.

Where it *still* beams deep color that had so enticed us *then*. Moist sheen rising from each bloom despite the brittle parchment of its drooping spearlike leaves, the coarseness of its woody stem. "Tall Ironweed" (name we still love) that many years ago I ceased to water. But instead, in whim, have circled our "small Stonehenge" with each beetle-husk or locust-shell, each new bird- or rodent-bone, gathered on our daily walks – together and alone – over the years ...

So long *intact*: a purple throb escaping its full bloom; on darker mornings spread plum-black above the twist of ragged foliage. Or like the coal-blue sky of evenings before "certain" rain (that *never* falls or fades to silver mist), *stopped* the moment when I'd stripped it from that mother-plant with some unthinking swiftness like the pure stroke of a sword. Never now to fade to a light mauve or milky pink (colors paired with cute frivolity), nor wither into fur-brown nubs – as the living do mere days beyond a rich ephemeral bloom.

Somehow stopped. Remaining *deep* forever in that moment when I'd clipped its stem of "rusty iron" from the mother-plant, beneath those high umbrellas of ripe scrim and lancelike leaves. And witnessed, gazing through them to light sky and fluffy cloud, a piercing contrast I still feel! Serious *iron purple* with its hard-brown *woody* stem – "Iron Purple": oxymoron of my need ... streaked with long abandoned webs, like ageless wisps of hair, upon our floor.

Earthy whisper we attain to on each flowerhead, that will not wither to brown nubs, nor fade into mere nothingness as we both age and know more who we are. Long after water vanished from its vase.

Dried stiff but boldly luminous – a purple with such character to verge on deepest blue or black. Yet still most surely purple (knowing truly what it is) – ceaseless glimmer above crust of leaf and stem, a sharp but fragile silhouette against our off-white wall. Crisp *now* as the day I'd stunned it into chemical shock, like pure arrested thought, some eight years back. Uncanny glimpse, defying time and common sense, of color setting firmly into wisdom, unexplained.

Dan Stryk

DOLPHINS AND SUN STAR

Moving in tandem, south to north,
between Grotto Pizza
and the gazebo
at Rehoboth, but out there a bit,
dorsal fins high (they're close
enough to see with the naked eye),
while at 6 AM on the upper level
of the hotel deck a man with binoculars
and a woman chat
about Big Sur on the other
side of the country and a jazz singer
who was splendid last night,
put heart and soul into his songs
totally. And the woman says
she's been coming here for twenty years,
and her words, how "the dolphins
always pass at just this time,
maybe the *feeding* is better now,"
find an echo with me
when abruptly,
a gauzy ribbon of cloud ignites to flame
in that borderland
where sky and ocean meet. I look out
at what transforms to ...
(even as I, too, trans-
form, become one with, if only
for an instant) that fireball, huge, consuming ...
And then (almost, it seems, against
myself) I pull
back, eyes glazed,
still *wondering*, scan the waves
for those dolphins.
They are all gone ...

Mel Belin

THE PARABLE OF THREE DEER CROSSING A FIELD

Every three or four days they return.
Waiting motionless in the wood's edge
beyond the wall, testing the air, vaulting
suddenly on stiff legs into the field.
Walking knife edge single file through
frost killed grass and golden rod,
stiffening a moment at the gravel road
then crossing, quicker now, to disappear
among the pines.
                                        I have never seen them.
I would not commune with Nature
through the shedding of their blood
or eating their body's bread. I want
no eviscerated Icon-head upon my wall.
I have only read their gospel of tracks
in the gravel.
                                    I receive only the testimony
of the fruitful grass bent aside
by their passing. For relics there are
only a few hairs caught upon a thorn bush.
I have never seen them. I do not rise early
to peer from my window.
                                                        I do not conceal myself
with foliage or grass to watch them or
to take their photograph. I have no need
to prove their existence. So they are there
always, like Gods in a myth. Like love
among men. Like food, fire, and a companion
at the end.
                                They are a presence
in the air. Bent grass, tracks a bit of hair.
Signs of a presence. Like Gods in a myth.
Like love among men. Like food. Like fire.
They will be companions at the end.

Robert Chute

THE IBIS FINALLY SENDS BACK HER INTERVIEW ANSWERS

1. Guess the name of the next hurricane. I thought Hugh should've been named Lizzie.

2. It's okay, except for the heat. The heat glazes everything. Some afternoons, the pier looks like it'll melt and fold into the sea. Sometimes, even the sky turns dark yellow.

3. June, 1981. She was afraid of needlefish, howling about how they looked like knives.

4. That's difficult in one word. Well, when she'd pass something on the road, she'd lean out with anticipation, like she expected to see a dead cat. When she'd figure out it was only a curled strip of palm tree trunk, she'd slump back in her seat, like she was let down.

5. Yes; especially when it's a good day for a song.

6. Six o'clock in the evening: when no one's in the water and sting rays bend it into ripples; when sand on the shore turns gray and cool; when all you hear is herons huddling deep in the mangroves.

Bianca Diaz

Through sweat I look up from digging
in hard red clay. Trees look back at me.

Dean Blehert

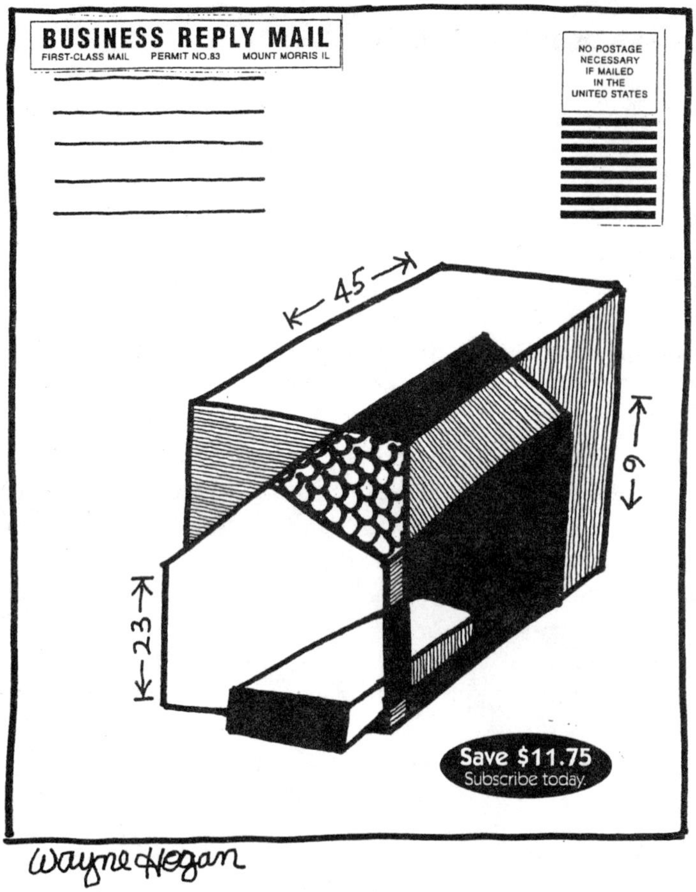

EPOXY

Dark evening
in an empty glass.
Shadows rolling
down the hill like onions
in a skeet field.
Buzz words flying.
(Buzz words flying solo.)
Collaborative thing, "epoxy."

Wayne Hogan

THIS MACHINE WHICH BEGAN

There was this machine which began
with a low hum but kept getting louder
shaking tables   cracking windows
breaking nerves down   and everyone said
it couldn't get any louder
because it would break itself down
but it keeps on getting louder and louder

There was this iron axe which began
chopping   chopping   chopping little sticks
and then bushes   and small trees
and big trees   and everyone watched
and said   it couldn't go on much longer
because there wouldn't be any axe handles
but the head keeps chopping   all by itself

There was this hammer which began   tapping
tap   tap   tapping   but kept hitting harder
shaking the ground   crushing rocks
smashing houses   and everyone said
it would have to stop very soon
because of the second law of thermodynamics
but it keeps right on pounding and pounding

There was this blood which began to drip
like an iceberg melting   and dripped faster
and faster   like a glacier thawing   and blood
ran in rivulets like Spring was coming
and everyone said the world must stop bleeding
because of cybernetic controls in natural systems
but blood keeps flowing and the grass is red

There were these poets who began to write
small words   joy   peace   dove   child   love
and they kept on writing till they ran out of paper
and they wrote on walls and stones and trees
and everyone said they would have to stop writing
because there weren't enough words in the world
or places to write on   but they *kept* on writing

Robert Chute

WHITE TREES IN THE DISTANCE

a white wind of
petals, maybe snow.
The longest I've
been so closer to
you on the sheet
of paper. Like your
death, these poems
about you, a wild
surprise. The last
page in the note
book, still I think
I'll need another
notebook before I
can let you go

Lyn Lifshin

(Borges non-fiction, selected)

23&24aug03 Sandia Mountains

has this trail looped back around
or
should i double-back?
seems almost an hour ago i left
            the main trail
following that sandy side canyon
up to this ridge where
this older trail appeared

summer and we're in the middle of a drought
and so is my water bottle

does this faint trail go anywhere at all?
these piñon are much larger than normal
cactus huge as trees
boulders big as houses
i am unsure where i am
bushwhacking
expecting snakes in the overhang
it's cooler up here at 8,000 feet
vanilla ponderosa in the air
pungent
i'm going to need rain gear in the next hour
clouds forming
i can't find my pen, must
have dropped it after the second stanza
i wanted to write some of this down

Mark Weber

SNAPSHOT

At night, a man is sitting at his desk in pain,
aging, full of dreams & fears, till Jessie
barges in & nuzzles his left leg & says, *Hey,*
you know that open box of milk bones in the kitchen?
Well, I've been thinking ...
The man washes down another vicodin,
scratches the dog's head, & the two of them
get up & leave the room. When he returns,
he sees how dark it is outside, & late.
He types & stops, looking for a phrase he can't
quite find, some gesture that the past
had given him & taken back.
Above his desk, that ancient snapshot of his folks,
two Lower East Side kids, their lives together
just beginning, who will never understand
that everything the future holds for them
has passed. Dexter Gordon's lush & melancholic
take on "Don't Explain" drifts quietly
across the room, as if that saxophone knew,
somehow, that the fellow staring at that photo
had been weeping, stupidly
& over nothing. At the keyboard, Sonny
Clark looks over once at Dex & nods, & shuts
his eyes, & listens to himself – to both of them.
Staring out the window at the dark,
the man finds, he thinks,
at last, what he's been looking for, & goes on typing.

Steve Kowit

DO YOU REMEMBER THE BLUEBIRDS? II

If you sit still you will melt like cheese on a burger or the ice sheets raising the
tide down at the harbor the last few years
like an octopus a magnum opus is tip-toeing its arms forward
as the Red-belly woodpecker chomps fat outside the window
where yellow leaves rain down each one waving
early dark long nights stumbling up dark stairs;
how the artist is pre-disposed to manipulation of necessity ... trying
to find a little strength and time to put forth paint, words, what-ever.

Joan Payne Kincaid

BIOGRAPHY

So I'm writing you this book,
the good, the bad and the ugly.
My mind spins, this is not a
photograph.
That's it. The poetry is it.
Interjected, I say.
The quiet street below my window
in the dead of night.
My papers in neat stacks.
The darkened lobby down the stairs.
I pray the elevator does not
get stuck while I am in it.
The people I have loved
and who love me.
That's it. The poetry of it.

Tom Bilicke

LIFE RECORDS

Accountants tell us we should keep records
and they mean of course tax percentages
estate contracts, salary fluctuations

I'm much more interested in emotional statistics
the actuarial tables of lived lives
indices of the honorable struggle
files for caring and nurture, audits of the mostly worthwhile

also the red ink stuff, pages of summed pain
columns of cooled intimacies, the failed familiar
human availings too late but anyway tallied

the warehouse of human dealings never closes
the little data of mortal endeavor
what grand collation of human enterprise
such splendid inventory

Tricia Cherin

I DO NOT REMEMBER WRITING THIS POEM

September 21, 1978

your eyes
        entering my own
leave little shade

but a bite of sun
        to lean on

and mystery to saddle
when a misshapen
            pony
        glides by

Sue Abbott Boyd

THE VISITORS

– for Ann Darby

They stand without pity or shame
like tourists on the bridge to your next
great sadness. They have been walking
in bad shoes. They want a cold beer.

They've come with their one small
suitcase, and night's implausible
laundry list. It's late.
They're tired of being poor.

All day the wind fails them, so does
the sky unloosening its sullen
Esperanto. They know the hard
currency of coffee and cheap cigarettes,

the accidental prayer of rain
on a car roof. Priests of indecision
and poor judgment, they reach into
the ancient dark to pull a coin out of thin air.

Call it a gift, a simple benediction,
as they move tenderly through the door
of your best life, whispering
Take it, it's yours. Write this down.

Silvia Curbelo

ST. JOHNS RIVER, 1972

We could start here, with the over-
the-backseat slap, a too-full moon,
the stench of rotting river vegetation

or not. We could start with something
nicer, supposing there were memories of
hugs and smiles, or happy
family meals that didn't
end with scraping chairs
and shouts,
cold food thrown as punctuation.

Let's try this, instead: the father
standing by a fence in moonlight,
stroking the long nose of a dark horse,
pouring beer into small pools
in his palm for the eager
horse to lick away,
while the daughter watches
from a distance she considers safe,
marveling at this display
of near affection.

Debra Bokur

THE NAMING

It all began with Mother,
Mother who called me *nui*,
word meaning female, meaning daughter,
gave me a doll to cherish, made me
addicted to tidiness, driven to fulfill
each commitment. She spoke of an imperfect world
and women its caretakers, how bulls were
like men, responsive to the gentle
tug of a nose ring, they run
from sticks and hard voices.

My husband Joe names me Wife, meaning
lover, caretaker, mother of children,
keeper of his faith and lineage, gives me
the lamp to light his way home.

Now my daughters name me, believe
I am everything, ring me with needs.
In their faces, I see the past
and future, time rippling curves of faces:
grandfather's, mother's, Isaac's, Joe's they rise
and vanish like the wind's breath on water.
I accept their naming. I am kin
to Poet Chu Yuan's self-drowned body
nibbled to nothing by river fishes.

THREE SERVICES FOR THE COLLAPSE OF THE LIVING ROOM CARPET

On the night of a full moon in September, walk alone through the city streets or a country lane. Pretend you have no name. Pretend the wind has no name. Pretend the trees have no names. Walk as long as you want. Walk all night if you want.

*

Keep a small mirror by your bed. Every morning when you wake up, look in the mirror and say to yourself, 'Who is this stranger? I have never seen this person before,' Then give yourself a new name for the day. Do not tell anybody the name. Give yourself a new name every day, but never tell anyone your secret name.

*

One night when there is a full moon, get a bucket of water. Take it out into your garden and set it in a position so the moon will be reflected in it. Lean over the bucket and look at the reflection of your face as long as you want; then dump the water out of the bucket and onto the plants in your garden.

Marlene Kamei

THEN YOU HEAR IT

dogs wake you at 4:00 AM
needing to pee, you walk
them to the shared backyard –
overhead: a waning moon; white
patio lights, like errant
stars, spill over the neighbor's
wooden patio railing

instead of returning to bed,
you sit on the round planter
made of cement bricks, rosemary
pours out in arcs from each
triangular opening; the scent
reminds you of someone, you
can't remember who – only the
cloying sense of being too-near

then you hear it – deep bass
from the upstairs' window, laughter;
you envision another full recycling
bin, Wednesday's thunderous release
as the garbage man dumps beer and
wine bottles into his humpback truck

dogs watch you suspiciously
as you remove their leashes, tell
them to run beneath the moon's
quartered-face until their haunches
ache, their tongues, covered in
spittle, slide out their mouths

bass goes deeper, people
begin dancing – some sway by
the window in coupled-silhouettes.

others move singly, possessed
by the rhythm of the
hour, by alcohol's loose fit

as the sky lightens to that
peculiar shade of off-blue, you are
still perched on the planter, still
head-tilting, foot-tapping – the dogs
settled at your knees, all three of you
lost in B flat, scented in rosemary.

Colette Jonapulos

MERIDIAN WITH NOCTURNE SUBTEXT

Toward noon the blue circumference of heaven
I count on mornings to hold the day in place
scatters mid-August across the face of clouds
which assemble and rumble, dispersing my attempt
to find a human form, gods, any image.
And then it is the old haunting begins
to heal the wounds I carried half my life
from a family probably no worse than yours,
reader, my parents, my mad sister living on
through old age, bound together, their nursing home hell:
father, mother, sister circling circles each knows best.
Writing this down has drawn me from myself, reader.
Walk with me as I talk: the night sky will be clearer.
I can pin the stars up there if you're here, listening.

Peter Cooley

NAMES OF THINGS

In children's own way
they make fun of a father
who cares for trees, flowers,
names of things, like chicory,
box elder, mullioned windows,
serendipity, lilac, privet hedge.

As a boy the scent of a privet hedge
would linger those nights he walked
the springer spaniel through the park.
He never knew then what that scent was.
Now, that scent echoes with the sound.

Only later we understand,
all things stir echoes;
like the roar of ocean in a shell.
Each name is a wave
that bends the breath.

The other day they found a mimosa tree,
its leaves blushing at a finger's touch.
He spoke about its peculiar charm,
"Why is it so important?"
the children asked.

The mimosa's wild beauty
reddening in green summer
leaves roots of memory.
Mimosa, serendipity, privet hedge:
these names of things –
the entrance to our stories

Peter Krok

AUDEN ON YEATS
(with 2 lines from Yeats, 1939)

a voice
        and how to use it
for the free man
        how to praise
and use it
        in the prism of his day
for the free man
        "to undo the folded lies"
and use it
        how to praise
in the valley of its saying
        and use it
a way of happening, a mouth
        and sing
"and all I have is a voice"
                    O, yes
teach the free man how to praise

John Elsberg

IN THE AIR

Sometimes our memories
stretch so thin
even the lightest of birds
can't perch on them
as they go the distance,
feeding on the faint hum
of a wiry voice.

Duane Ackerson

Wayne Hogan

WHEN THE STONES ARE SILENT ...

I am seeking out the town
where my grandmother came
to convergence of despair and hope
on the same forward-thrusting day
after being hungry under gray winter sky
yet another morning.

I am asking corners
of abandoned Abbey walls
if she leaned against their rough surface
for a shy, clandestine kiss
one adolescent dusk,
asking dark-paneled pubs
if the little girl of her might have stood
beyond the smoky pane of stained glass in the door
gathering courage to enter and fetch her father home.

This string of quays might be the spot.
As the tide pulls waters of Lough Gill
out into Sligo Bay, the gulls say *maybe*.
A pair of swans glide toward each other.
Slender necks interlace into a knot
and extend skyward to embellish the letter
beginning
Here.

Maureen Tolman Flannery

A MAJOR EVENING WALK

Best at the end of dusk, the lights on inside, always little lamps; beige shades or resin-ish, like the ones Frank Lloyd Wright used to like, always a fireplace in the older houses, a painting over a sofa, another one over the fireplace, always a wall full of bookcases, books, a huge TV, some viewers, the houses themselves, Tudor half-timber or Cape Cod cottages, Swiss chalet, ranch-style/Prairie-style made out of huge concrete blocks, huge old trees overseeing everything, clematis and snow-balls, wild-grasses tamed around rocks in the front yards, the older the neighborhood the better, always someone sitting on a front porch, there's David Stowe, "Hey, David!" "Howya doing, pal?" new book on sacred music just out from Harvard, then another block down Steve and Angie Elliston who I know since the University of Illinois days fifty years back, "How about a little drink?" "I'd better skip it tonight, just back from Montreal, overdid it a bit ..." "The next time, then ... you owe us a visit!" Steve laughs.

My right arm around Bernadete's waist as we walk along, the hills getting steeper, the houses fifty years older, past our old house on Forest Avenue, the second oldest house in town, Fred Graham's son on the front porch with his wife. "Howya doing?" "Grreat ... only my father had another heart attack." "Terrible!" "Oh, it's not so bad, had another stint put in, that's his third now," "Tell him to give me a call when the mood hits him," "Will do," down to Beaner's now, my wife with her decaf coffee, me and my Sprite/Sierra Mist, we share a rich dark brownie, hellos to some familiar faces, then back into the almost-total dark, *really* foresty now, bats out, the moon, bats and cats and almost time for the evening news, *Lach Heim*/To Life, my head starting to fill with dead grandmothers, parents, cousins, friends, wishing there was a hill I could walk up and there they'd all be there, a little Irish Creme and Egyptian style crunchy walnut-chocolate cookies, embraces all around, even if your hands pass through them, and the cookies and whiskey are pure imagination because there's no more bodies out there any more.

Hugh Fox

REFLECTIONS ON THE MASTERS

for WHC 1/06/04 RIP

Watching the Arnie Palmer
crossing the bridge to

the clubhouse for the last
time after two rounds of 18

missing the cut but getting
a standing O for all those

memories provided; 50 years
of hard work, skill & performing

under pressure, as gracious in
defeat as he was in victory

& I thought: if my father were
still alive, he'd be watching too.

Alan Catlin

MY NEIGHBOR IN HER VEILS

Somewhere when she was a child on long slow
afternoons she licked persimmons,
crumpled saffron in her mother's kitchen
of garlic and plums, her flesh camouflaged
even in the heat, dreaming papaya seeds
sprout in her belly to grow a skin doll.

I think of George Segal in his father's butcher
shop despising the stench, daydreaming
gauze and veils, of wrapping the flesh
chunks dripping blood in white, still as a
nun, quiet as my neighbor must have
been kneeling on stone, swathed like a

nun in yards of cotton the sculptor could have
dreamed into marble. Now in a new country
far from canaries and blue limes, mocholelos,
in a town where she can't find good cayenne
or fresh turmeric, where people stare at her,
their eyes dark beads she can't see her reflect-

ion in. She brings the car into the garage
on weekends to wash it without her veil but
some late mornings when everyone's gone
from the house she runs barefoot, her hair
streaming down to the river with green pasta
for the geese whose wings flutter around

her, make her feel she is back in her mother's
house beating quilts and pillows, their harsh
cries more soothing than English.

Lyn Lifshin

RUDIMENTARY

Yet, what if this muse so unexpected
turns crooked smile to her final lesson –
that love is or is not more than friendship

to enlighten, foil and fool her again:
lost sailor, content to sail without ship,
because soul is not starving, already bled,

like a bruised slave inured to master's whip,
done with desire, certainly passion,
although shadow knows heart in body not dead.

There's bewitching sight, sweeping pelican
or sun over horizon, mystic blood,
begging sharp tongue touch her, not wet lips.

Does ghost now appear, haunting what is fled,
to remind that wine taste is only sip
for woman who would never cage wren?

Or is phantom wild pony stealing nip
to possess rainbow of the color red?

Rochelle Lynn Holt

THE PASSPORT

I've always wondered
why the Kaiser
came to this village
shortly after the turn of the century.

My father comes to the house for a noon meal
old hat shielding blue eyes and ruddy cheeks.
Horsemen march through the town
pushing peasants to the side of the road
so their dust won't touch the royal car.
I wonder how the Kaiser likes riding through streets
in daylight so the opulence of gold braid
and insignia on the coach could shine.

The people murmur, and then become silent
as the roar of the carriage approaches –
groaning as though an entire Empire rides on its engine
Near where my father stands the car halts
and the Kaiser rises, unafraid in this remote place.
He throws gold coins to the crowd
and my father picks one up.
The old man sits down and the black car
rumbles into action flanked by stiff-necked guards.

I wonder what my father thought as he held in his hand
the passport for his entry into a new land of sun and wheat
leaving behind sabers and plumed helmets.

Marie Asner

ROOT SOUP, EASTER MONDAY

The soup cries out for roots: turnips, parsnips, even a clumsy rutabaga. Again we test the scumming broth of Easter's turkey bones in my copper cauldron.

But this is spring. Saturday I cleared out stones, planted seeds, cubed potatoes rife with sprouts, buried them in one last row.

Then the news came. My father just died.

Tonight I mince last winter's parsley with garlic, onions, cabbage, bay leaves from the Christmas wreath.

My father often told me how a soldier, young and hungry, asked shelter from a peasant babushka.

"I have no food," she warned.

Then from his pack he took a pebble, dropped it in her pot. Soon their soup was bubbling with unearthed miracles of vegetables, one strayed hen. They ate all week.

Tonight Ann offers carrots, David – two potatoes, Sergei – beets, and calls it borscht. I throw in onions, garlic, Jerusalem artichokes.

"Each guest is sent to us by God –" an old Caucasian song my father sang.

Now our soup pot simmers high as it simmered in his house, overflows into our bowls. He must have willed a stone to me.

Elisavietta Ritchie

EVOLUTION OF WINGS

My father sees cicadas walk
and frowns – *they're*
bottom-heavy and slow.
He knows lizards, mosquitoes,
frogs, common beetles. As a boy
in Havana, he'd spread honey
on his arms to attract fireflies
and they'd come, alight on
his glazed skin and stagger
their way up and down, flicking
their green lights on and off
like pinball machines.
                                        To have
seen my father do this, to know
this boy's thrill at the quiet
thrumming of tiny wings
as they took off – the kind
of ascension reserved for
green, near-elastic things.

Bianca Diaz

THE BEANPICKER'S DAUGHTER LEARNS TO READ

The world was flat, an endless bean field
stretched to the corners of the sky
farther than I could see. Bound by such sweet
black loam, myself no taller than a grown bean plant, I
had no cause to imagine more small brown humps
speckling the horizon like Braille – my
aunts, uncles, cousins, bent like anthills over green.
My mother tied me to her leg with string
so I wouldn't fall in drainage ditches. No shoes. Our feet
dyed themselves black, toenails, everything,
for years. My only hat my thick black hair.
If I peed in my pants, the pitiless sun
glazed me dry. Under the spell of that squat green sky
I could hold my shit the way a man holds tears.
Crops here, crops there. We could not tell
when winter came. I sat three months in little first grade chairs –
four times, four states, almost learned to spell.
The pages dazzled me with hieroglyphs; I could barely speak the language.
Sometimes a bright picture would roar inside my head,
though I almost always mixed up "dog" and "God."
But one day in Belle Glade at season's end
among the lissome beans – I was now ten –
the words exploded in my head like Christmas pinwheels. I read one word.
As sparkles drifted from the green crown of winter air, I read
aloud one whole three-word sentence in inglès
and the round world opened up to me like los brazos des angeles
and here I am.

Chick Wallace

MRS. WEI IN AMERICA

In the House

Ants bite my heart when I am alone
in your house. Picture windows invite thieves,
Our houses are safer. Padlocked

iron gates, barred windows, broken glass
on wall ledges keep robbers and salesmen
at a respectful distance,

At the Safeway

The food wrapped in such clean paper,
so many colors! The clever shapes of glass
and plastic. I want to take your containers home

to Malaysia, impress my neighbors.
American meat has no smell. The water
tastes strange, even after boiling.
I'll be glad to be home where foods smell right
and I can argue with the butcher, get an extra
ounce by calling him Miser.

On the Road

Everything here is big, especially the roads.
Cars and their drivers are polite.
Back home, eight tigercars would have squeezed

into the space between this car and the next,
their drivers giving you the finger
for tamely waiting in line.

On Governments

Malaysian Government is like the American
price system: take it or leave it.
It's easy enough to leave a dress hanging

on the rack, but a country is not something
you can get up and walk away from. Your Congress
resembles our marketplace: haggling and shouting

until everyone is a little satisfied.
Can we visit a shop where I can talk
the price down? I want to buy a victory.

I need a good fight.

Hilary Tham

WHAT DO YOU DO WHEN YOU CAN'T FORGET THE ONE YOU DON'T LOVE ANYMORE

Somewhere in the night   water is bending its knees
listen to the beeps & voices on the road or just
stand at the little attic window late past midnight
& not quite hear what the neighbors are saying as
they come home noisy   & slam car doors

it's not Cezanne shouting to his models   "Be an apple!
Be an apple!"   when he arrived he came   from somewhere
else   as a legend might   in a boxcar

Maureen Owen

OUT THERE

Those questions that are used to take the measure of a mind – what are they? "What day is it?" "What year?" "Who's President?" Well, like-minded questions, you could say. Questions any self-respecting mind would have to resist. And the questions will be too loud because they'll assume diminished hearing ... or perhaps they sense some cloud, no, "fog" they'd say, a fog they have to penetrate.

He gives them a crooked smile. He is amused. Particularly by "Where are we?" He seems to be so in his own place. They stumble into more personal questions, seeking an entry to the world that could be behind his smile. "What kind of work did you do?" Again the smile. He has decided to give them a piece of their world. He says, actually whispers, "Trees." He was Tree Warden of the town for most of his life, can claim to have planted and fostered the beautiful trees for which the town is known. He is uncurling from his shapelessness in the chair by the bed. He sits up straight, a delicate rack of bones.

"When I was a kid I worked for my father in the junkyard." His voice is so soft and slow; he must work for breath. "But when I got back from the War there was no money in metal, so I ... trees."

Impatient with the slowness, impatient to connect, they talk about how there can be very good money in junk, but junkmen are likely to poormouth their business. Claim in even the best of times there's no profit.

"Swifty" he whispers. "I'd hire part-time help for Spring planting, for spraying, and for cutting and clearing off-season." They strain to hear. "Lobstermen mostly. Bob Swift. Ronny Merriam. I'd ask 'Gettin' any lobsters, Bob?'" They are counting every word.

"He'd always answer 'Nawthin' out there, Bill. Nawthin' out there. Nawthin'.'"

Shivaree

WEATHERING

You told us about chairs
made for out of doors,
rough-hewn and left outside
so the joints could fill and grow
together in the rain.
These chairs could last fifty years
on the front porch, you said,
and fall apart
with a year of the parlor.

Watching you at dinner,
tan face, knotted arms,
your wife pale as fresh cut timber,
I could see you knew
what sort of carpentry
you were.

Duane Ackerson

THE LIGHT HAS FEET

Mrs. P leaned over to Mr. P and said,
"Through the Venetian blinds it looks like
The Light has feet." Suddenly she knew she was a poet. Yes,
It was becoming clearer to her. Just yesterday
At Friends of Pinecrest Auxiliary dinner
Didn't she say the cheesecake tasted *heavyhearted*?
And there was more to prove she was a poet. She never felt
She was quite where she really was. Things
Went through her like a screen door. Breezes came and went,
And didn't matter since all the things you wrote about didn't get read
Anyway. And the people you wrote about just died.
The literary life sounded good in a notebook but it felt
Like high heels that didn't fit. She posted poems
On the bulletin board every day but someone
Always needed the thumbtacks.
Being a poet felt like getting to the mini-mart at four minutes
To four when it closed four minutes early.

And she knew tragedy. Oh yes. Just this week
She clipped coupons for food she didn't want to buy,
Then forgot to turn in the coupons at the cash register. Irish soap,
Frozen Chinese, fake meat. God knows what all
Sitting on the shelf staring like expensive eyes.
While she sat staring back like parsnips without butter.

Mrs. P was only happy when it was time for chapel.
Then she could take her mind off herself. Nice,
They had church everyday so no one had to worry what day
Sunday might be. She liked to dress up too. She wondered
About that nipple jewelry they talked about on TV. But
Why bother with new things.

She had such pretty earrings her sister brought from Scarsdale.
The earrings were not in the shoebox, so she knew she must have them on.
If pepper was already sprinkled on the egg, the salt must be there too.
Since the pill was not next to the water glass, she knew she had swallowed it.
If that was a man in her bed, he must belong to her.

In the chapel, they were going to sing "Blest Be The Tie That Binds".
She liked that. She thought unhappily that cheese binds too,
But she always sang anyway.
It made her so glorified just sitting in the hard pew at Pinecrest.
Everyone alive, sitting and standing. No one dead.
Just the thought of it made her want to wake up the old man snoring
And tell him '*the light has feet*'.

Grace Cavalieri

EURYDICE

"I went to Ghostland last night, got past the first two old women, through the cloud-pass, I could see the Ghostpeople up ahead sitting around the bon-fire, I could just barely make out his face, he looked up, saw me, I could see him form the words with his lips ... 'TO-MOR-ROW' ... then I woke up, the mailman had just put the mail in the front door slot ...."

She was eight-two, white hair, white skin, when she sat on the white damask sofa in her living room she disappeared.

Hugh Fox

A TIME IN SPACE

An old stalk of a man
passed me midday unto *a sly grasshopper the*
straw of him(the old stalk of a man)still
blazing a little bit of sun as he saw me
this side of a hill coming home
and our encounter was quite proper
tho purple and I discovered how age
is not a burden one lies down but lifts up
and heard *silken apple pure speech* almost rock
me to meet my lover turning home and I thought
of how good truth really is facing situations
truly is most fortunate and left on a
midday hill an old stalk of a man and an hour
of myself ticking against falseness the second
hand of me revolvingrevolvingrevolving.

Sue Abbott Boyd

AFTER MANY YEARS

Now   words of his
spaced   darkly
with a   nonetheless
of   lily white

a piety   for
men and   gravestone-
landscaped
memories

sprung   from a
templed mind   which
once   was friend
to me

Hans Juergensen

UN TITLED

A bird has built its nest
next to a charged telephone wire
chirping like a first time bride conceiving
an imaginary child
There is no vertical
                    horizontal
just the immediate intimacy
                    of the now

A.D. Winans

GIFT OF PARADE

After the box-silence confinement,
she went out to gift of parade
where baton twirlers tossed confetti,
and drummers with high hats played.
She bought a sweet-scented pine,
some tinsel and miniature lights
to bring stars into empty night,
her dark cell of cave.
She began to write letters,
use her telephone, meet people
as walls of Geraldine crumbled
to let in fresh air and musical rain.
Oysters in shells feel no pain
or deep well of refreshing dive
into swells of humankind
that somehow appease suffering.
Away from her rocking chair,
she learned how to dance
in pure light of flowering day.
She touched ice without fear
while laughing like child
who skates on frosty mirror
for first time in winter.
Geraldine discovered motions' reward,
pleasure of devotion to her self
removed from gray closet walls.
She was romancing life,
riding a yellow bus into the city.

Rochelle Lynn Holt

SMITTEN

The woman sitting in front of me
on the city bus had mahogany hair
that fell in brushed cascades
to her shoulders.
It would have been enough
to be her son, and that she
sit on my bed in the late afternoon
and read me stories.

Tom Bilicke

revelation

on icy road
you change your mind

no one knows
your destiny

nor why
you are shoeless

the earth is flat
you've found the edge.

Spiel

Maybe romance dampens some young roller blading socket falsely draped down into samisdatz and plain text. Ovals of us lord it over shapeless ones. I feel the heat rise from my face. I feel semiconductor penetration chill the mercy side of thunder, and I thrive on cinders maybe once and maybe forty times. *Bring me hazelnut decaf.* Roasted warm round summer in the blood of us. The leaflets dropped from sky. A used-car moderato once forlorn. In triplicate the form melds reason with the bread. Some ransom notices occur to me poetically when I seem no more than a gland to partners. Freshen this. *Use things you have the moment that you need to use them.* Things change. The discreet things. Planned things. Flocked small goslings become ... what? Amendments of their own.

Hunters relaying their finds to gatherers, vests made of cloth like supple fur, less soft though, and a string (gratuitous) of pearls

The alfredo of it all, sweet merchantly, a pleasure to sit down

Define *fallow* without using once your hands

Sheila E. Murphy

DEARBORN NORTH APARTMENTS

Chicago, Illinois

Rows of rectangles rise, set into brick.
And in every rectangle, there is a lamp.
Why should there be a lamp in every window?
Because in all this wide city, there is not
enough light. Because the young in the world
are crazy for light and the old are afraid
it will leave them. Because whoever you are,
if you come home late but it looks like noon,
you won't tense at the click as you walk in
which is probably only the heat coming on
or the floorboards settling. So when you
fling your coat to its peg in the hall, kick
off your heels, unzip your black velvet
at that odd vee'd angle as if someone
were twisting your arm from behind,
then reach inside the closet for a hanger,
just to the dark left where the dresses live,
what happens next is a complete surprise.

Lola Haskins

ALL THAT GLITTERS, SHIRLEY

Breezy, matter of fact, unflappable, and naturally sympathetic, Shirley had the gift of putting people at ease. She sat down to breakfast one morning and said, "For what it's worth, I've been thinking about becoming a charlatan."

"Shirley you're not serious," a hundred voices at the breakfast table deplored. Shirley continued to eat her waffles, dripping syrup with every bite.

Slowly, very slowly, she stopped eating breakfast, and it was obvious to all that she was going into a trance, Shirley.

Her voice, when she spoke, changed timbre, no longer recognizable as Shirley. The dialect was of a time long past, only heard, if heard at all now, in the movies, or on the boards. A real live dead person, she sounded like.

The charlatan that was Shirley straightened up and brushed a damp tendril of hair from her forehead. A disembodied voice intoned, "Allow the soul of a mournful wretch to weep a moment at y'all's feet."

"Shirley, for God sakes!"

Unmindful, the voice continued, lamenting in heart-broken tones, "I'm past the age for pistols at dawn."

"Of course you are, Shirley! Of course you are! Now stop this nonsense. Right now!"

"You're all right, Shirley," the hundred voices said. "You're back with us."

And that day, the day their Shirley became a charlatan, would become the stuff of legend.

James Mechem

CHAMBER MUSIC

last night at the chamber music concert
in my blue blouse and matching ring
short of a choir there were soloists

in a Bach Cantata a ringer cellist home run
touch time-line but there was a lemon

in the trio out-of-time~ too silent clone
tangible in the rear section lost ... out-
on-a-limb lusting for home, a cellar

to melt into to come Schubert a-roaring
contralto's caramel sugar scale haunt

hunting a shoe her leg slant string notes
at the core of things basically cool catch
camisole scream bust-y thrust bounce.

Joan Payne Kincaid

PLAYSCRIPT

How still Manhattan was
that morning.
Odd that workmen made no racket
cars rolled noiselessly
no heels clicked on the hard white floor
of an empty waiting room.
No sound at all to interfere.
All Manhattan just a backdrop
for our starring scene.
A sharp dog-bark, bus-driver calling
"You two ..."
But they weren't real,
just props.
Nothing real but you and me
hands, lips, faces touching
and now the intermission
real enough, in a noisy world.

We have made a new art form:
a play with intermissions
longer than the acts.
Whatever is to come –
what climax, dénouement –
whatever may be written in the script,
one scene was beautiful.

Carolyn Sobel

COFFEE HOUSE IMPROV

They are so into it
they are gone,
flying like my fingers over paper
in the heat of poetry.
I could listen all night
to pure bongo, electric guitar.
There is nothing to say.
So pure they have to stop and ask
if this is cool.
So pure I tell them
they don't need words.
They are masters.
I bow in silence.
They are playing for me.
They are not playing for me.
I could listen all night.

Herb Kitson

EXAMPLE

Exercise every muscle
Xylophone practice twice a day
Another year mastering scores
Many children still play jumprope
Playmates have monkey paws
Leave my Saturday toys untouched
Envy true musical dream Brahm's EXAMPLE.

Eda Casciani

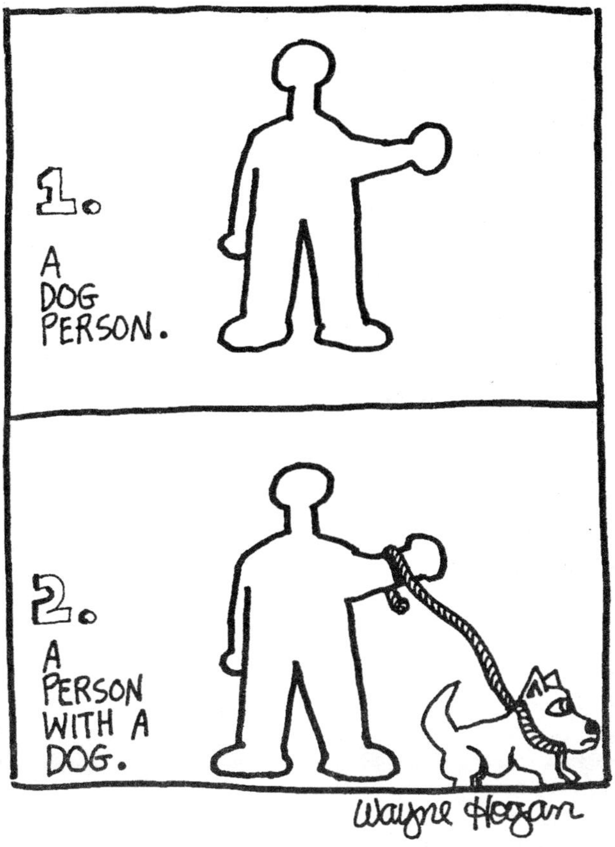
1.
A DOG PERSON.
2.
A PERSON WITH A DOG.
Wayne Hogan

THE WHOLE SHOW

He'd been there
the whole time. The
dog, too. He'd
thrown the stick and
the dog had chased
after it. The stick
struck a nearby tree
and caromed off
in another direction and
at another speed altogether.
This was a physics with which
he was not familiar. He
wished his dog hadn't
seen this.

Wayne Hogan

VIRTUOSI

She attacks the keys, aggressive, furious –
it's Beethoven's *Für Elise* –
at her feet, the dog howls, G minor.

Thalia Xynides

JONQUILS CAN HAPPEN

Three cats – taken off guard –
slink into the monochrome
A song invades the quiet street
decomposing into objects
vibrates from out the frozen steps
leading upward to
a smile hanging there among the
trees in the familiar garden
and the familiar serpent
Jonquils in dusk
can happen
They pop like crackers
snapped by Christmas children

You are subject you are object
You are dreamer
and dream
Doors are all jars
The smile cracks slowly
to let in the clamoring
stars.

Fanny Ventadour

WU WANG: INNOCENCE

It falls out of a tree into your lap,
an acorn, a windfall.
It leaps from the shaded fence
and tears your sleeve,
catches you unprepared, sudden:
dinnerbell, junebug, laughter. Ice.

Ann E. Michael

BRIGHT MOMENTS LAKESIDE

A derelict, half-hidden boat house,
rusty pump house, and a long flat causeway dam
rampant with summer grasses. Cowpads,
a few crows lifting off them as you walk.

Bright moments lakeside: flickers, wrens,
chicka-dee-dee-dees (they like to hang out
with titmice). A bullfrog – two frogs – leap
from the duckweed (I don't see any ducks).

Color coming awake – yellow, orchid,
magenta – in cinquefoil, smartweed, false
strawberry, Dianthus or Deptford pink,
alfalfa or cow vetch (such confusion
in the common names!). Two or three
kinds of clover, two or three kinds of bees.
A cedar and scruffy shrubs crowd
the low barbed wire fence along the dam.
Back toward the boathouse, pickerel weed
rising up out of the shallows

floats its purple-blue flowers on emerald clouds.
No one much sees this, I guess. Only
the locals who come in pick-ups
across the fields at evening, who climb
up here with cigarettes, chips and six-packs

to wait for bass and bream. And the cows.
The hull says *Arkansas Traveler*. Dented
and camouflage peeling and two seats broken,
an old aluminum boat nuzzles the dam.
A dark green board and a coffee can
soak in the bilge, dragonflies ride the gunwales.
Oar locks, but no oars.
                                A jump-rope painter.

Peter Klappert

TRIPTYCH: CELEBRATING APRIL

crotch of a crabapple
        three blue eggs
                in that nest
                        we thought abandoned

field of wild mustard
        two blackbirds
                how green these rolling hills

perched amid
        shaggy somber cattails
                there!
                        scarlet cardinal

Susan Weaver

PLATTE RIVER GIRL

Some people say there's no magic in dirt, but they're wrong.
Magic is everywhere and if you eat it, you'll take in
a little goodness for your crops.
You'll come to some reconciliation with life
and the products of your endless suffering.
Mostly we just kill those who claim to know,
who take in our dirt and pass it through their bodies.
But we're wrong in this and we always pay
for taking away the one good thing that may come to us
in a generation.
The trick is knowing how to recognize when it happens
and holding on for dear life.

Laurel Speer

THE FISHERMAN IS OLD

He navigates as a stranger
the contraptions of his own tackle box.
Each time now he must master anew
the tricky skill of using his own reel
as the line balls up and tangles and confounds.
With infinite patience he unwinds
what his palsied fingers continue to enmesh.
With his few remaining teeth he bites
a lead sinker tight around the line,
squashes a grabbed grasshopper
onto a hook he can hardly see,
shuffles to the water's edge
and is a happy man.

Maureen Tolman Flannery

THE BATTLE

Whiskers and bits of line twitching,
He waits, eyes my bait
And waits some more.

I see him there. Dark phantom
In the green-gray water.
I wait, pole in hand.
Today.

I wait some more.
Shoulders and arms begin to ache,
Muscles frozen,
Poised for action.
Hot!

I'm getting thirsty.
The shade that was has moved
Leaving me exposed
To the Kansas sun.
Maybe, not today.

I stabilize my pole.
Walk back for a drink of water.
Just as I raise the jug
I hear the snap.
Broke my line again!

I sense laughter
In his satisfied slap.
We both know, even when I land him,
I cut the line.

Dorothy Jenks

FOUR MILE CREEK

Ours is a quiet porch.
Westward dark mountains
Offer mysteries.

Nearby the creek murmurs.
Canyon winds whisper
Still only trees hear.

Dorothy Jenks

PRAIRIE SONG

In Kansas, you cannot tell where the plains stop
And sky starts. They merge, marry over the horizon's lip.
Disgruntled Mormons first laid their claim,
Warring rattlesnakes and coyote packs.
Here that vast expanse of high grasses reaches on,
Searching out forever. Here we are homeground,
Braced, digging in, burrowed into root cellars,
Readied for tornado alley, when churning winds
Descend by skips and hops, snatching up trees,
Barns and sodhouses, howling with unleashed glee,
Depositing stranded cows from their pasture
To three farms away. Only the hearty survive
And thrive, here. Only strong dreamers put down
Deep roots. They nurture cottonwood groves
And Chinese elms, soybeans, oceans of wheat.
Here in Kansas, sunset is another gloaming prayer
Where scorched gold and flamingo pink
Join with French lilac and I am blessed
To surrender gladly to the lonesome winds.

Virginia Love Long

song roots

dark deep in us sounds an ocean drum
in an inward valley copse flute   a finch
and a thrush. winds pluck a rainbow harp. we
are never without primal joy.
                                        blue skywings
transport us into joy-deeps of nearness. we
can go far in   to rediscover ourselves.

how hard we try   to smother our inner songs.
how we strive to turn our drum only
into furystorms.
                    black holes are not our
ultimate soundless sounds. we have known joy
in the wide risks of waking. the demonic
whirlblasts burst out and under with new
beginnings, sources of fresh drums
and songs.
             we do not need, we cannot, to
wait: our flaming dusts carry what   is known in us
deeper than pain. drums and song, shorn and shattered,
outlive fury, even god's. that dark whirl, penetrating
down, sows our knowings in a beyond-time waking.

song stirs deeper than lips and throat, drum

beats further in that blood. rejoice

and know, in every soulsound, is a reach
beyond

Will Inman

TAI: PEACE

When is sky under earth?
Reflections in a still pool.
A bounty of winter blossoms –
the small things rise and go.
Heaven and earth change places,
unite at the water's edge.

Ann E. Michael

COMPOSITION

Towards the end, his left hand became paralyzed, and during that period he wrote a beautiful piece for the left hand alone.

– Mrs. Frederick Converse

It sings clearest which is nearest sleep.
The halfway child, humming to himself.
The old woman, thinned to a piano string,
who remembers suddenly the flash of green
she saw when she was six, and not again.
Of the remaining hands the right dances
in the air. The left holds still.

This is a piece for the left hand.

Lola Haskins

Icy rain outside.
Warmest thanks to whoever
invented inside.

Dean Blehert

FLUTE

The orange grove is stunned by the moon
oranges change to enormous opals
leaves to electrum foil.
The whole grove glitters.

In the exact center of the grove
sits the albino snake charmer
playing astral music on his bamboo flute.
But the cobra is old and lethargic.
It too is stunned by moonlight
and the cold fire in the fruit.
It lies unmoving in its wicker basket.

The flute notes rise and float above the grove
and half way round the world the sea serpent
hears under the black tons of ocean.
For centuries he has not stirred.
Now his heavy coils unwind, slowly
he starts swimming toward that grove of opals.
Soon all the seismographs on earth
will record his movements.

At this precise moment you,
asleep in your high city room,
will turn without waking
and all your long cool naked body
dream of the albino snake charmer.

Evelyn Thorne

FROM THE PORCH IN ALMOST DARKNESS

before you can see
more than the lace wake
the ducks' v makes
on polished water,

rose petals,
brown edged,

light as moths,
clot in old leaves.

What's left of the moon,
a lobe of honey,
smears dark satin,

geese honking
light back,

goose music

Lyn Lifshin

unseen guest

bullsnake at my barefeet
coiled and sunning

I regret that my presence
compels her to inch away

til she disappears
now I find myself

frequenting this doorway
longing for her return

Spiel

LIKE EVE, I MUSE ON HERPETOLOGY

I too like lizards, their climbing, clinging skills,
how they seem to sleep till time to nab a bug
or sprint quicksilver-swift and disappear.

At six I bought chameleons at the circus.
When they escaped, I hoped that God did not
change them to snakes, but let them grow

to crocodiles ... In Malaysia wary *checheks* caught
our insect hordes. I later rescued blue-tongued
foot-long lizards asleep on Outback roads.

In Maryland, observing blue-striped skinks,
still I watch for miracles of metamorphosis:
a lizard stripping limbs, transforming to a snake.

Were I Eve, I'd munch the apple, beg the clever
lizard for another. Ignoring risk of severed limbs
he'd not regenerate, a change of lifestyle for us both,

he would oblige me with a peck. Yet he'd not lose out
on paradisiacal joys: Look! Behind the boathouse
two black snakes stretching from a burrow hole

entwine long necks, while unseen beneath the ground
their remaining lengths are copulating sinuously
unencumbered by octets of legs, or any sense of sin.

Elisavietta Ritchie

4sept03

i just vacuumed a bug –
i'm not happy with myself –
before i vacuumed the bug
i was fine, but now
i have questions about my character
big questions
not that i'm one of these sensitive poet types
i've been known to punch fellow human beings
it's guys like me who start wars
we're a mess
you invade my space and
i'll vacuum your ass into oblivion
why did i do it?
i was vacuuming the rug (here come
the excuses) and he was there
and my evil twin did it
now
i wonder if i should dismantle the machinery
and rescue him?

all over our yard we allow black widows
to live, it's a sanctuary for one of
the most poisonest bugs on the planet
(Janet's sister in New York City says she
intends to wear a ghostbusters suit next
time she visits)
normally i escort the bugs out
of the house in my cupped hands
now
my evil twin is taking over

Mark Weber

THE PERFECT CRIME

My husband's second weakness
is food. Lots of it. I've started
him on a special diet. A pound
of bacon for Sunday breakfast,
eggs cooked in fatback, buttered
bagels, a side of hash browns
with grilled onions, Smithfield
ham. I stir my tea over toast
and smile. Slabs of ribs with fries
for dinner. When I roast a chicken,
I stand back to let him lift the skin
before I carve. He's ordered a new
neck size for his oxford shirts. I've
started buying beef on the hoof,
whole milk, frozen onion rings,
cases of beer. Now when he slips
in at 5 a.m. I no longer pounce,
out of bed, search his pockets,
smell his breath. Instead, I roll
over and plan the day's menu,
a dozen donuts, sausage
pizza with double cheese.

Linda Rocheleau

THEY DON'T SERVE MARTINIS IN HEAVEN SO I'M NOT GOING THERE

What gets you through four-thirty afternoons nodding on tiresome failure ...
the cat's puke the dog's endless resentment for distant trails not taken;
the poems that needed polish leave you wondering what the hell happens
to a day ... words in the pre-lobed cognitive void hearing the Cardinal storm
in at seven while the keeper studies his bum foot forcing himself to be
older than he needs; you are dressed to *perform* not experience ... price for
poetry and painting you could have met a woman who knew it was possible
to own a pretty place and care for each other toward the end. But you
needed words and canvasses a long time ago when everyone left for college
you sat in the dental office writing checks and developing paranoia in a dark
room of x-rays when the town knew you should be singing in some opera but
all your teachers manipulated dependency and now you perceive the birch
leaves move into the room and blow late May and there is no place you would
rather be, listening to birds, drinking Lap sang sou chong tea a teacher taught,
or a martini sin when the sunset is crackling gold.

Joan Payne Kincaid

TOO LATE THE HELIOTROPE

Thorns etch with arabesques of sighs
viridian
the night obsidian
the graven bird with swift stiletto eyes
looks down
on howling fright.

Too late the heliotrope of why.

Someone
pulled the tigered trigger
in a wry and withered
sky.

Fanny Ventadour

WATERING THE GARDEN

At first I regarded it a chore.
Now I savor it, desperately
needed relaxation, a respite
from the squirrel-cage of thoughts,
a sudden listening to all that is there.
Birdsong once more more awesome
than the most intricate flights
of human-wrought fancy available
on vinyl, more delicious to hear
than even the most foresty woodwind
passages in Dvorák, Sibelius,
greenier even than Delius.
Suddenly the mockingbird alights
once more at the zenith of
the Norfolk Island Pine,
its throat no less melodious
than Keats' Nightingale.
Announcing itself to the universe
more eloquently than the most "trained"
opera singers, more poignantly,
more jubilantly. Wingèd aria
Out of the Cradle Endlessly Rocking
apparition. Do I Wake or Sleep?
The Bird Sang Me. Beyond Word.
Trills and runs beyond notation.
Watering my garden and really breathing.
Time out for timelessness. A "breather."
A brief reprieve from a life
sentence to "urgent concerns."
My breath and my heart reunion'd
with the wilderness

snuck up on me in my own backyard,
my spirits rising indomitably as
the 15-foot purple hollyhocks
springing beside my garden
in southwest San Francisco,
emerald hummingbird
come to hover holyghostly
in the rainbows of my hose-spray.

Jeff Poniewaz

ALWAYS LESS

What our hearts
To human happiness
Yield is always less
Than the full moon
Yields to an October lake.
up there, down here,
All my ideals
Begin to sound
Like former allies.
But what I allege is this:
Ten minutes alone with you
On one broken boat
Under blurry skies and
Faint galaxies
Is worth ten thousand
Years of
Unbroken
Promises

Sander Zulauf

coyote's sermon from the chicken coop

someone had died and the people called on coyote
for a sermon for a discourse for anything he could offer
and coyote told the people that life was struggle,
real struggle, and that struggle was beauty
and the people struggled and were not satisfied and
asked for more and coyote told the people that the only
secret beyond existence was non-existence and that if
they would contemplate that they would achieve
immortality and the people contemplated but still
were not satisfied and asked coyote for more
and coyote told the people that the word is the truth
and the word is a lie which makes everything true
and everything false and so the people talked among
themselves and were not satisfied and asked for more
and coyote told the people that time could be conquered
by the space of the mind focused and the people focused
their minds but were not satisfied and asked for more
and coyote told the people that the key to the
strength of the soul was in sacrifice and so the
people sacrificed but still were not satisfied and asked
for more and coyote told the people that everything
depended on cutting loose, standing above, and
being free and the people experienced liberty but
even still were not satisfied and asked for more and
coyote told the people that he would give them one
more truth, and that was always be in love always be
drunk with love always be so drunk with love that
nothing else matters and you will live in the eternal
moment and the people were satisfied

Tony Moffeit

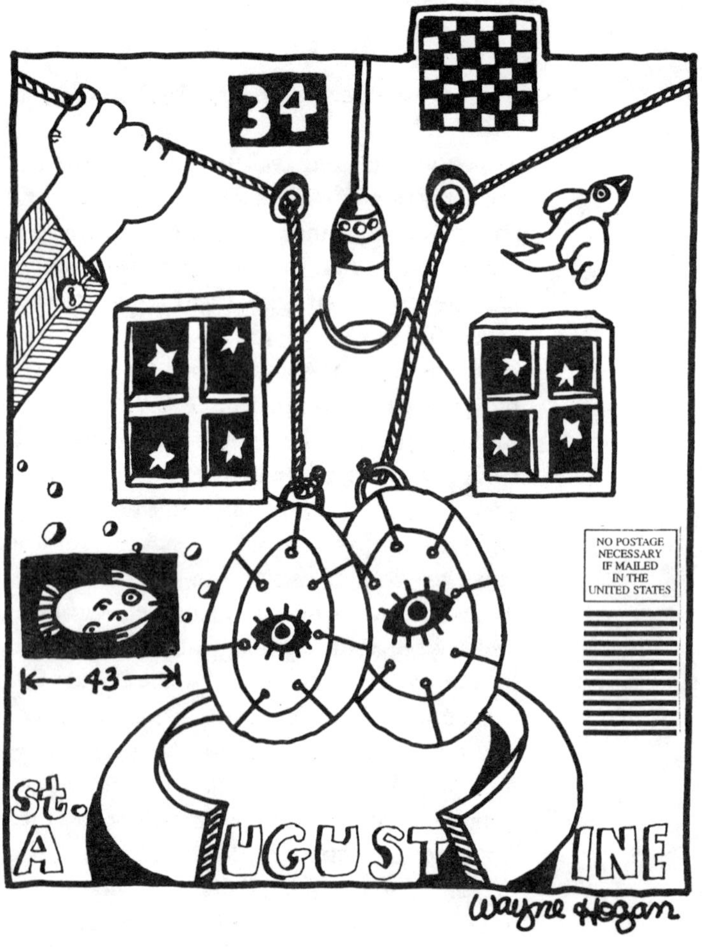

from:
"TIME OF TRUTH"

... Perhaps it is
best that we hold our tongueforks,

eat the potato salad
prepared for the occasion;
it is so eggwhite valid.

Sue Abbott Boyd

INDIAN SUMMER IN ATLANTIC CITY

A man, scooping ice cream to passers-by
in shorts, has an *I can't believe*
this good fortune hope I have enough look.
Storefronts boarded over,
un-board, even as I feel transported, outside of time,
or to another strand of it, distant, luring
in this city of Monopoly ... The arcade barker's cry,
"C'mon over, c'mon in;
anyone can play, anyone can win!"
How we tossed the dice
as kids, laughingly innocent. Circled our tokens 'round,
built houses and hotels then on properties,
whose names still resonate – Marvin Gardens,
Pacific Avenue, Park Place, and the like ...
Only now, a woman in a long flowing dress reaches
her personal *Go*, leaps into the ocean breakers,
still bracingly cold, near a surfer in a wetsuit.
The cloth, soaked, molds to her body;
her laugh,
exuberant, infectious as if to say,
the Hell with metaphysic November,
which lies somewhere between the man,
footless, armless, playing a keyboard with his mouth
"hang onto your hopes, my friend ..."
and the black woman – a Salvation Army of one
in this land of Beelzebub with his casinos –
her voice rasping, "we should all return,
we should all repent."

Mel Belin

MIAMI

I take a walk along the side cement between lagoon, canal, or bay, and the sky rise hotel and monoliths of condominium chock full of shelf space and rich seniors. At the end of the line segment I locate a small restaurant that serves lox in many forms to no one near my age but me. The other customers talk in small groups or couples about lunches they have known. Nineteen years ago today I wore a flowered dress, performed a flute recital. I lived in a dorm room and rehearsed tasks that I did not understand. Today I am not responsible. Nearly forget the name badge on my suit. Waitresses keep saying "Sheila" and I think them prescient. The rhythm of my walking is a drug. I like the thought of lying in a hammock healing. Running down Squaw Peak wearing a pair of tennis shoes with grips. I'm being paid to think of little else. I'm being paid to resonate with nothing. Tasks practically have antlers. It is the germs I am concerned about. The way they sneak in when thoughtlife is raining. Bleeding customized humidity again without surprise.

Sheila E. Murphy

CENTRAL STATION

Playing Bach in the glass construction
sewn into an iron frame,
a flautist paces the traffic of the masses;
adagio, allegro, allegretto,
and every costume has a face
beneath the sparrow trapped inside.

David Chorlton

DINNER ON THE HOTEL PATIO

This patch of sky/a pink
petal drifting over
prairies/hushaby
the passionate lips of leaves
licking patent leather air/
we peer at one another like
poetic people should
the movements of passersby
windless/the pretty waitress
weightless/and time pauses
beside our table like a patient
husband who absentmindedly
discovers his wife.

Sue Abbott Boyd

ANDANTE LOVE

We are not a ripping *scherzo*,
not *allegro* of vibrating dance,
certainly not *presto* crescendo.

No, you and I are *andante* –
lingering over espresso and
creamed strawberries at dusk,

andante, sometimes *tremolo*,
in soft, swallow-butterfly swoops,
con brio, sweet on the tongue.

Mary Sue Koeppel

NITOBE GARDEN

The stillness of this place rings in my mind.
As water falling softly intervenes.
Each bridge has been so carefully designed.
I wonder what "Kasuga style" means?

As water falling softly intervenes,
I watch a giant koi glide through the pond
And wonder what "Kasuga style" means,
As sunlight turns the leaves from green to blonde.

I watch a giant koi glide through the pond.
Five squadron ducklings splash-land into view
As sunlight turns the leaves from green to blonde,
They have their aerobatic drills to do.

Five squadron ducklings splash-land into view,
Their sudden entrance celebrating life.
They have their aerobatic drills to do –
Like household chores between a man and wife.

Nitobe's gifts cannot be praised enough.
Each bridge has been so carefully designed.
Whichever path I chose, stone smooth or rough,
The stillness of this place rings in my mind.

Jill Williams

DEBRIS

yesterday
I walked the beach
of the Villas
gathering debris
when I started out
it was only
an unbroken tiny pink pearl shell
a small quilled sea gull feather
a blue clawed crab's pincher
& the back of its coral rimmed shell
but then there was
the grey tipped gull feather
& a baby horseshoe crab the color
of iced coffee with cream next to
the piano player on South St
on Sunday morning
soon my hands were full
& I wanted more
the numbered dock floats tangled
in marine rope
& then
a blue & yellow coil of rope
when I lifted it up
I found it connected to
seaweed & salt grass
by a fishing line
only for a moment
did I think of untangling
what I wanted from
what it had become attached to
then I knew I couldn't
the attachments formed in the debris

of this shoreline were
what I had grown up around
I could no more untangle
the fishing line
from the coil of colored rope
than I could untangle myself
from a foghorn's wail at sunset
sandbars stretching out long
at low tide
the weathered wood siding of Smitty's Bar
or steps to the sand
swept away in the last storm

Kyle Laws

POEM

the heat splinters like a worn reed in your hand.
you find yourself thinking about her as you take long
walks that hug the shifting edge of the sea. hidden
by the shadows of the breaker rocks you watch the
driftwood ride upon arches of foam. there is no moon ...
only the lights of distant boats you feel yourself
drifting towards. the seaweed clings to your skin
like breath. shells cover your ears and your eyes become
white stones of salt. everything you taste is blue-green.
you are happy when each of your fingers break off
to become fish

David Dunn

ISLAND OF THE OSCILLATING FANS

remains isolate, desolate & un-
occupied except for this surfeit
of oscillating fans – some mounted
on large poles carved as totems
with smooth blades wide as windmills;
box fans with protective gratings
removed propped on flat beaches
held in place by sea coral, conch
hermit crabs may enter in doldrums
times, though leaving is another
matter; window fans in framed from
drift woods, deadfall, spinning blades
airing rooms without walls, ceilings,
only sand for flooring; industrial fans
housed in metal forms dropped at
random along the tideline facing up,
huge motors, gears, all moving parts
suffering an accumulation of rust,
ocean weeds, dune sand drifting;
all these fans with power cords
removed oscillating with the prevailing
winds, singing of the shrill beauty
of a haphazard muse.

Alan Catlin

KISS

On the patio of that little cafe in the Del Mar Plaza
across from the Esmeralda Bookstore, where you can
sit sipping latte & look out past the Pacific
Coast Highway onto the ocean, a couple is tangled
in one of those steamy, smoldering kisses.
His right arm coils her waist, arching her back
& drawing her toward him. He could be Sicillian,
or Lebanese, with that gorgeous complexion,
those chiseled forearms, that clutch of dark curls.
The young woman's skirt, lilac & sheer, lifts
as she stretches, levitated out of her sandals, out
of her body, her head flung back, fingers
wrapped in his curls. Her long chestnut hair
spills toward her thighs as she clings to his mouth,
to his loins, to his chest. How wickedly
beautiful both of them are! To their left,
off the North County coast, on an infinite sea,
two sailboats triangulate heaven. In the sheen
of the morning, you munch an apricot scone
& sip your café latte, that blue cup of light at your lips,
with its genie of steam. In its vase, on your table,
a white tea rose shimmers. Your fork
shines on its plate. Everything trembles & glows.

Steve Kowit

WHERE WE LAY AND MADE ANGELS
(Evening in Antigo)

That town
where the new bridge fell
into the icy river
and made the nightly news in Houston
fourteen hundred miles away.

That town
where a new turn light
caused Aunt Tillie
so many accidents
her son hit it with a twenty-two.

That town
where big bucks
strutted down main street
and young men saw the fawns,
shot them anyway.

Where the angelus
chimed 6 am and pm
and old men faced East
and crossed themselves

Where sounds
hung in the snowfall
and waited till echoes
floated down to the blue snow
where we lay
and made angels.

Here on the broken bridge where
water slips around
snow-covered stepping stones,
the moon on the darkened river
fragments and tilts.

Mary Sue Koeppel

APRIL

Here's the morning: wrong train to Ausburg,
cruel stranger at the station, moment of regret.
Later, good tea, not the weak stuff at the hotel,
but deep black, redeeming. Next, the ticket checker
smiles, her long blond braid sways with each
rounding of the track. Because she's not offended
by my accent, she can star in my hit movie, not
yet written, the one about the girl from Frankfurt
who saves the world with kindness. Later still, something
sweet, with berries and a little cream. A long walk
alone beneath the mossy trees, a good soft bed,
a pillow spewing real feathers. Here's how it ends:
four kisses, blown in each direction, bright
graffiti on a bridge across the Rhine.

Debra Bokur

"I Love Barbie Taylor. T. Mc."

– sign spray-painted on a since-demolished wall in Arlington, Va.

It's official now. T. Mc. no longer
loves Barbie Taylor – not for the commuters
on I-395 who for eight thousand yesterdays
read passion in three-foot schoolboy script.
Today the bulldozers came, and romantic
words became rubble, to be cleared away
for the ritual mating of asphalt and earth.

But what of *real* love? Did Barbie and T.'s
live past demolition, or die long before it?
Did T.'s love leave the wall? Was Barbie's ever there?
When Barbie laid azure or emerald or onyx
eyes on T.'s declaration, did she roll them
in ecstasy or embarrassment?
Did Barbie and T. find out too late
that love can squall and soil itself,
or wither in a stranger's wink, or survive
the fatal screech of cars against each other?

Or did Barbie and T., a couple not perfect
but comfortable with their familiarity,
see their wall come down with a pang for youth
so long gone, so shortly gone,
hold hands for the millionth time, and wave
at T. Junior walking with his first girlfriend?
If the earth has an answer, the dozers drown it out.
Their burring voices shake the overpass
where "Todd Loves Tiffany" appeared last week
and echo in the park, rustling the oak tree
where Isaac has loved Maude a hundred years.

Miles David Moore

WELL ENOUGH ALONE

My home is furnished by former lovers

A tapestry from Carol eighteen years ago
(you were with child and I was full of ideals)
books and records from dead Kathleen
(we were to meet by the water when we were old)
cut blue figurines from Ruth and a burgundy clock
(we made love in the sand your kneeprints are still there)

I am a lucky man
paintings by a poet and her ivy ten years old
a wooden table a bookcase a frayed coat candles
this mobile this mobile from a woman
I only knew a night or so it is clay and consists
of fifteen seagulls (one was broken in the mail)

And lately a tape deck from sweet Marie
who shared the Caribbean the brown pelicans diving
I still play your music when my mind goes white
(I think of you more than you could bear to know
now and then I shiver over the empty sea
of the future and all we threw away)

Oh but sometimes I consider how my life is furnished
by vanished lovers I walk by my rooms feeling lonesome
but so enormously fortunate through every doorway

Frank Johnson

STRANDED

"Two rides for the price of one,"
the marina operator said as he
looped a harness under the bow
and slung the boat onto the rail.
He warned me about the shoals
as we rode out far enough
so the motor could be dropped overboard,
but as I headed deeper
into the uninhabited coastline
I wanted to see what
I had never walked along,
so I turned into the shore
until the motor stalled.

I'd hit a sandbar,
and had only one oar to maneuver
since two would have been useless
against the currents, he'd said,
its main use to raise a life preserver
as a distress signal,
but after having been told *not* to do
exactly what I'd done, I could hardly
raise a signal to the circling plane
pulling a banner for Whaler's Cove
and admit my foolishness
having grown up on this bay.

The next day,
sitting on Washington Street in Cape May
holding a photograph of the wrecked Sindia,
the woman beside me puzzled how the ship
could have gotten stranded off Ocean City.

But I sympathized with the captain
of that long ago sailing vessel,
glad there are not pictures of me
still being sold, riding in circles
with a chipped blue oar
as I backed into the tide
one ripple of the sandbar at a time.

Kyle Laws

THOMAS TAPES

Under puff cloud rounded sky
in the drab smacked middle of a played-down life
I Dylaned a day with his sonorous voice
and voweled up the void in me
scooped hollow all the dulled-by-duty years
full of sackcloth sound
and blacked out lines in widow's weeds.
The dreadful never-dead bellowing of him
verberated up the dried in, tried off
too long relied under sayings that behaved gravely
while his leapt headlong and time short
into souring memorial of sea lapped sound.

Maureen Tolman Flannery

NESTING BOXES POEM

Once my student, she sends me celestial tea, scents

shimmer	BOX OF DREAMS	even before
boiling water	I have a secret hidden	prickles of spice
	deep within a blue glass	
rise, ovals	box of dreams, a waiting	with a sense of
	quest that calls me	
cinnamon	to some hidden, sparkling shore.	exotic
silken	I lift a leafy, scented blossom	a fabric, woven
	to my lips and breathe.	
wordwise	My dream expands. Now I feel	a moist
reminder	the sun upon my face and see	soft, in steam
	it glimmer	
we were	through the branches, laden	learning then
	with the heavy fruit	
together	of possibilities.	odd lessons
	Earthbound? Hardly.	
vanilla and	I fly with my belief in everything.	
nutmeg	My dreams are portals.	jungle vines
	I have learned the treasure	a jingle
	of each moment –	
copper	and I know the sound	and other
pearls	that sunlight makes as it rests	marvels
	upon the branches, as it	all gifts, given
	settles, with the years	
reminders	upon my cheek.	relics
	Debra Bokur	

in small boxes, like words holding worlds, say to me survival's a grace.

Ruth Moon Kempher

LAMPLIGHT, YOUR HAIR

Lamplight, your hair: things are just what they seem,
A room with space and objects preoccupied.
I touch your face, but cannot touch the dream.

Facts flicker us; time's a stutter, not a stream.
The future is a room where we once died.
Lamplight, your hair: things are just what they seem.

But suddenly – I don't see any seam –
The room becomes your smile, and I'm inside.
I touch your face, but cannot touch the dream.

Time stands still, quick! caught in the eye's caught gleam,
But space keeps coming; on its tide, twin swans, we glide.
Lamplight, your hair: things are just what they seem.

Time's a transition in a freshman theme:
Consequently, as it were ... When words collide,
I touch your face, but cannot touch the dream.

Only by dreaming now can we redeem
A future no man waits for. Time and tide.
Lamplight, your hair: things are just what they seem.
I touch your face, but cannot touch the dream.

Dean Blehert

BRUSHSTROKES AT DAYBREAK FOR THE YEAR 2005

Does one return to sleep to learn the outcome of unwanted dream?

Early light's susceptible to infinite arrangement
as the lines dividing darkness from its loss dissolve

into the painted strokes that follow sleep,
blend substance with opposing moisture

against a measured surface of particulars,
thus transcend the comforting familiar

of uneven surface taking in each line,
that traces lucent mink across a swatch of silk.

A child's first thought does not find text,
and lives apart from sheltered comprehension.

One thinks to brave another conscious moment,
as if a frost, about to be relaxed, induced a form of being.

What is loved remains to be held open;
sense of sight indulges in perfume

releasing the exactness of a foreground
in favor of affection that absorbs a warmer touch.

Sheila E. Murphy

THE PLAN FOR TODAY

My Saturday coffee is lukewarm
but there are three ripe blueberries this morning.
I'll take the good with the bad.

My love dashed away early
but the rabbits haven't eaten our lettuce.
The day promises to be bright and sweaty.

The lessons of the morning
are strewn throughout the house,
their subtlety piled for later celebration.

The goldfinches are interrupted
by my 12-year-old's call.
We'll rendezvous at the stable.

Where has the sun of dawn
journeyed to now that it's 10:00 a.m.?
Somewhere a symphony is tuning up for another show.

My songs return from another century;
their smiles are worn but their grip is strong.
Between them the cicadas applaud.

My love will return home before evening;
our daughter will stay with friends.
I'll sing to them from the steps.

Tom Plante

deceit

we live
our lives
in mirrors

(confident)

our reflections
will not
bleed

Spiel

THINKING IT OVER

People ask me now that
I've taught the seminar what
I think of Hemingway. Well,
if he doesn't have the final
answers, he has the questions.
How can you remain true to
experience? How many ways
can you be manly? What is the
plan of the Universe? Who
will write the honest sentence?
Freud's What do women want?
His: Where is the Garden
of Eden? A Freudian Eden,
the womb, but the mother he
needs is a substitute mother,
the Hadley or Agnes to whom
one does not owe allegiance.
A Horton Bay, for the swimmer.
The woods, where he could take
his gun. But I am no Hemingway.
I don't carry a gun, and I
quit competing with my father
for my mother. She was not
the All-American Bitch, but
a martyr, a secular saint. A
peasant genius. A child. In
her old age she read *Lord of the*
Rings, went to Beatles movies, came
to town and rode the bus. No one
like her in Hemingway. It took
education, higher, before I
could walk, talk, carry on
like him.

Robert Novak

BIRTHRIGHT

my natal horoscope declares,
"Your father will be able to
leave you *very* little."

when my father remarried & moved across town,
he gave me a little house on two acres,
the house I grew up in,
the safest place on earth,
where Mother's ashes are planted
and the remains of every pet
i ever loved.

this came with a lifetime of lessons by example
in integrity
and a work ethic beyond reproach,
an undeniable sense that i was loved
no matter what,
along with an armful of Hank Williams, Sr.
and Connie Smith records.

Astrology is a bunch of crap.

Michael Hathaway

MY WHITE BUCK SHOES

It must be 1960. I'm lying on a couch wearing my dirty, splotched
white buck shoes. I've been wearing these shoes – not exactly
these shoes, but this type – since high school.
And though I'm 20 and in college, it has never occurred to me
that I might be out of fashion or ridiculous or failing to grow up.

But psychiatrists notice everything, even if they don't know
how to think about what they see.
So on this day he says: "Have you ever thought about why you dress
the way you do, why you might wear those shoes?"
I glance at my feet, but nothing relevant or interesting comes to mind.
So I answer simply: "I suppose not."
If I'd known anything about myself then – which I did not –
I might've said: "I'm a different sort of person.
I live mostly inside my head. I'm always thinking
about something else, so I don't suppose these white buck shoes
or any other kind of shoe will ever seem very important."

He was getting at something.
He was trying to open me up, develop my capacity
for self-examination, self-insight.
We talked a lot about dreams.
He liked my poetry, too.
But I think he was a little put off by my feet.

Laurel Speer

LOVE BEADS

Kay and I were always Into something, were
Into Scrabble when we first met, had our
first fights because I knew more weird words,
and then, we were Into Love Beads, drove
every Saturday afternoon in Kay's '66
Mustang, our 4-year-old daughters wrestling
in the back seat to see who'd sit in the
front seat with us, driving down to Laguna
Beach to the Greedy Beady to buy bags of
sparkling, opalescent, baubling, bangling
beads, spending so much we'd realize why beads
were once used for money and then we'd
go home and make strands and strands of Love Beads
we gave to our kids, our neighbors' kids, our
husbands, me giving some to the go-go girls
at work and guys in the band, future hippies
who'd wear them defiantly with their bikinis
and tuxedos, and then Love Beads went out of
style so Kay and I got Into dogs, hers a
dachshund mine a Dobie, we got Into champagne,
Into tennis, Into disco dancing, then Kay
got Into camping and bowling, I got Into poetry
and grad school, Kay got Into working as an
auditor, I got Into working as a proofreader,
our dogs died, our daughters grew up, married,
had babies, I married a poet and moved away,
and today, all's left of my Love Beads is this
one scrawny one no one ever wanted that's
worth maybe a dollar, but still it sparkles
like new coin as it hangs across a glass lamp,
reflects 60-watts onto the ceiling and lace

curtains, money of my memories, little crystal
balls into which to peer past and present, little
Aladdin's lamps, granting you more wishes than
you could have ever dreamed to ask for.

Joan Jobe Smith

MOST MATTERS CAN BE IRONED OUT

As we talk this morning, Rhonda irons.
I can almost smell the steam rising off
the damp cotton, hear the press of fresh
creases in the dark work shirts worn by her
husband, the local blacksmith. He hammers
iron into banana leaves over the burning forge
as we cradle phones beneath our chins, trade
tales of our mothers. My adolescent appeals
often made across an ironing board
as I imprinted yet another of my Dad's
handkerchief's with a smoky wedge. Hers
spoke of missing the task of smoothing
wrinkles from children's clothes while
her arms lay still from the illness that took her.
Wrinkle free, water resistant, par-boiled existence
had not yet emerged, in our Florida homes,
where iguanas tight roped the clotheslines
and grasshoppers large as 10 volt batteries
studded the playgrounds prehistoric.

Linda Rocheleau

MARRIED TO THE SOCKS

My routine mandated I go to the pub right after work and stay until well after midnight. This was always best as the wife and I were not on the best of speaking terms for the past three years.

I would just come in and with the lights off, I would climb into bed with her. I'd be very careful not to break the soundness of her slumber. I liked to then roll over and press my back into hers. It was the last comforting vestige of our slowly diminishing relationship. I needed the contact.

Two years of this lingered on until one day I discovered it was the laundry piled up on the bed and not my wife. She'd dumped it there on her last night at home. Sorted out her stuff and left the rest for me. Since I'd been getting up before she got up and going to bed after she was long asleep, I'd been happy in my complacency ... married to a pile of dirty socks and couldn't tell the difference.

Robert Joy

OLD RECORDS

She kneels and ghosts herself home,
pouring libation from her laughter,
plays back a voice many years gone,
a mother-goose, birthday-party chatter.
And ghosts me, too, till I am blind
with the fuzzy tears of a teddy-bear mind.

William E. Taylor

JEWELED HATPINS AND DELICATE BLUE STOCKINGS

They found it
just south of the
Labrea Tar Pits. A
(blue) '57 Studebaker, still
in good working order.
The driver's seat had been
pushed way back and
the steering column tilted
as far forward as
it would go. The radio
was on, tuned to
KXLA, hot music all day.
A local robin had built
a nice little Lloyd Wright home
in the gaped-open glove
compartment, Danish
furniture and all. When the
passenger's door was unlocked,
jeweled hatpins and
delicate blue stockings fell out.
A Navy life-raft-for-seven
of World War II vintage
was found inflated in the trunk
when the trunk lid was popped,
a (blue) '57 Studebaker just south
of the Lebrea Tar Pits.

Wayne Hogan

FIVE WAYS TO LOOK AT BLUSH

1.
It is in the nature of the horizon to recline. It is in the nature of the sun, to take her every afternoon.

2.
The azaleas suddenly explode in all-over pink, like a woman who can't get her clothes off fast enough. *Bad taste*, sniffs Mother. Then, moving on, *Plant something else*.

3.
The cheeks of the old woman pulling a shopping basket are startled fuschia, as if some passerby has just told her she is beautiful.

4.
A ruby glint is secreted in certain feathered bodies. The young of these birds are more voracious than the young of other birds.

5.
You brush it on, as an artist might. Dim rose settles along your cheekbones, goes wild into your hair.

Lola Haskins

DISRUPTION WITH PRIMARY COLORS

On the outer edges of youth, Schoenberg
leaves banking for his mistresses of musical

notation and muted colors (purest realism),
leaves Judaism for Luther, receives near-

love letters from Kandinsky, whose visual
disruption with primary colors ignites their

collective stretch of thought – more freedom
than the startle of birds in front of my car,

crows confused by autumn's sudden descent;
one, then another sullenly lift themselves off

pavement, attitude of artists interrupted –
surge of two men toward the spiritual with

paint brushes: Kandinsky's sainted heads
(complete abstraction) float above Mary

clothed in yellow; a chinless wide-eyed Christ
in Schoenberg's somber browns on cardboard;

one of autumn's defiant crows hops over the
center line, halts traffic going north, then south.

Colette Jonopulos

footnote:

purest realism: the term Kandinsky used to describe Schoenberg's paintings.

complete abstraction: the term Kandinsky used to describe his own paintings.

IN THE LOCKED MUSEUM

House of sleep, house of a long winter,
what moves through these rooms
is the past, windblown
as any field and just as green.
House of light, of dust
trembling in cupboards, lifted
as a child's voice is lifted,
the plain syllables of regret
like piano notes locked
in a tin box for years.
House of secrets, whisper
of shards and leaves, of wind
that stirs the ancient garden
and blows the old lilacs
to ruins, their deep,
clear scent drifting across
the wet stones of the courtyard
where the young Schubert
is peeling an orange in the rain
and feels the juice soak through his shirt.

Silvia Curbelo

IN THE BRITISH MUSEUM

Fascinating and so odd. How the purest features of the ethnic arts observed there – in archaic stone, wood, bronze – recur, drinking tea or Pepsi. *Most* in going popular garb.

Yet one still sees a flaming sari, *kumkum* beaming from dark brow. The jingling wrist of tribal pride. Semitic skullcap jostled in the crowds. One sees their curious gazes piercing bright glass shields that frame, yet separate them from, their dwindling pasts. Odds are, already lost.

For moments, then – freeing the mind – one sees the Benin nostrils flare, the keen-eyed scowl of samurai (despite those flashbulbs trained on grinning kids), the fierce Semitic glower of those lion hunters, bows pulled taut, or whipping stallions through dark limestone's brilliant sweep of pain in the grand Assyrian frieze ...

So strange to watch them drinking tea or Pepsi, lighting smokes. Drowsy from long hours on their feet. Most in going popular garb – ballcaps, stonewashed jeans – despite the trill, like Babel's fall, of myriad tongues. There, in the cafeteria, become one incessant drone. There in the cafeteria. Between the Elgin Marbles' glowing march, and that hallway flanked by the ghostly stare of Cycladic figurines ...

Dan Stryk

MUSEUM WORK

We took Abigail Monday
to the California Science Center
In Exposition Park
which used to be called
the Museum of Science and Industry

In the Center is a lovely metal amoeba
that expands and contracts
with pulleys and levers
grand evidence of scale and ratio

And on the third floor
undulating DNA
life worms
in epic video

A chance to ride a bicycle
on a tightrope
breathtakingly rigged

In the old exhibits
California science was more quiet
the great blue harbor
changed patiently from day to night
as docks were loaded and unloaded

And the miniature trains whistled and smoked
in their earnest routes
across the whole top floor
the labor of there to here

Tricia Cherin

TWO SCENES IN THE MANNER OF TURNER

Norham Castle, Sunrise 1797-98

appears amid
lifting grey dark

shades in aspirant
tinctures of light;

in the cove at
cliff's edge,

a one man skiff
catching the wind

that carries last
scurry of morning

fogmist away.

Unfinished Dawn

Bright as
gold coloring

reflected in
shards of

broken mirror
glass-sun

peaks above
crested cove

distant light
house dissolves

with last
pale effusions

Alan Catlin

THREE PAINTINGS IN THE PHOENIX ART MUSEUM

I

Landscape of the Three Gorges, Yangste River
Lu Hui (1920)

As seen from a cloud
floating into the gorge, the mountains
pale as they rise
to the edge of the silk

while a river cuts its crooked passage
through them. Small boats,

speckled on the current,
bob and toss
as incidental to the scene.
They will be moored
by nightfall

when ink spills around the moon
leaving on the water
a silver path
beneath a paper sail.

II

Travelers Among Streams and Mountains
Wang Shanglin (1808)

On green waves of rock
the knotted pines
twist in accordance
with a secret directive.

As far as the altitude
allows, they grow,
each into its own
windy shape

while men
riding along the path between them
are gone

as quickly as the snow
on the dominant peak
becomes a waterfall.

III

Monkeys on a Pine Tree
Ni Tian (1910)

Two monkeys
with soft fur and long fingers
are weightless
on their branch.

They are listening.
They are watching.
Tension bristles

through their liquid arms.
Such silence as theirs

is like that of the brush
swollen with ink
the moment before
it touches paper.

David Chorlton

REEDS GAP

Coon scuttle in darkness head home from hiking
In Paleolithic trail haunt epochism inversion
Then down on the interstate fireflies going off
Black deep stop on the shoulder a while to see
Away from the high-speed passing headlight rush
Over fields screened by tulip poplars sycamores
Millions of them alive in their blinking galaxy

D.E. Steward

FROM OUR CHILDHOOD

Then because late autumn falls on our hometown,
the earth blackens with rotting apple
so sweet our noses swell and ache
whereas a breath away the hardening ground
will be the color of no color in our lives
by which is meant nothingness. From the school bus
the children burst forth toward the rush of the museum,
shivering to form two lines under the teacher's eye –
boys, girls – then to gape at dead lives encased in glass till dark.
We are among them, age six, even then observing them,
reader, my friend. Quick, button your peacoat up.
Look, I see your breath; you catch mine white, passing,
warming your palm. All afternoon, dazed,
almost asleep on the dead air indoors, we will troop by
"American Indians Attacking Fort Detroit" in chipping plaster
pushing us at closing to gasp dusk stinging our chests.

Fritz Kamp, Priscilla Housington, my cousin Dick:
all return to the bus tonight. Cancer, car crash, suicide.
The bus keeps emptying now as nightfall fills the windows
quickening disappearances of the world's beauty
we notice most at six: frost on the bus window
purple, ochre. Put up your hand to trace it. Years pass.
Now the bus slows more often. Oftener again.
Outside, darkness rises up around us, hurrying.
Soon something is slowing us at every stop, the dark
more beautiful each stop since all we see is ourselves
reflecting on the black glass, nodding, bent to each other.
Sometimes, our lifelines flattened there, our vision
fracturing with light, we think the bus is almost one with dark,
more beautiful because of it. Reader, we ride on.

Peter Cooley

TOLL ROAD

Long before he arrived at the toll booth, he was ready,
his two quarters separating, spiraling
into different trajectories of descent into the
wire basket. As he waited, impatient for the green
light to move on to another state, he thought: love
is a country where men do not ask for directions,
a country with tolls to pay.
What had they fought about? He couldn't
remember. Wind in his face, road unfolding
like a map full of empty places, as unknown
as the hollow spaces in his chest. This feeling of
loss is nothing, he thought, as shadows are nothing.
But his body knew otherwise – knew love was a
rope stretched taut between two climbers on haunched
shoulders of wind-scoured mountains, knew love
could freeze cold as craters on the dark side of the moon.

He could call her at the next toll plaza, say ...
what words were left? They had said too many
already. Listening to the rings, then her voice
"Hello". And without his speaking, she knew,
he knew, they knew, the silence humming
across the wires was the language they'd learned
skin to skin, knew the road home
had no barriers and that the door
would open to his hand.

Hilary Tham

REAR VIEW MIRROR

I look back, see myself looking back

Peter Cooley

DRIVE

Sitting backwards
in the front seat
thinking how
wonderful it
would be
to undress you
in the back seat,
lay you down there
on that tight
little bed
with windows
for onlookers,
your father
at the wheel
and me
driving like crazy.

Joseph Farley

THE GREEN AND BLACK SEDAN

My father's car
served him well
for years. When it was
thirteen he put

a new engine in.
At fifteen it showed
the first signs
of rust he couldn't

easily repair.
My father is losing
confidence in it –
he talks of scrapping

it soon. My father,
in his seventies, deals
carefully with
obsolescence.

John Elsberg

MAIN STREET

When our car checks itself into a repair shop
in a small town close the treeline
we pass the time
reading our way along Main Street
beginning with the crisp new banner on a lamppost
that shows three tulips and the local
auto wrecker's name; on to the faded cursive
at the Diesel Stop; in Wanted posted lettering
black on yellow, the Maverik
plstic moulded Country Store; hardware;
laundromat; speed limit 25; mobile park;
and finally the menu in the coffee shop with
mocha, latte, cappuccino, next
to the eye-patch mural of John Wayne.

David Chorlton

MOSS LANDING, CALIFORNIA

Moss Landing waits in cold fog just west of coastal flat artichoke fields and with its tidal creek and power plant it seems to lack perspective from within while its ultimates are somehow fundamental to the scale of us and our time alive. It's at the end of things and hangs with our awareness out there on the edge of the Pacific. Just past it looms the immensity of the beyond, the largest natural entity on the planet, Bora-Bora to the Sea of Okhotsk, Norfolk Island to the Bering Straits.

In close, the whine of generators' vibrative teeth-gnash high rpm permeates the low buildings, dirty windowed from the salt air, old fish sheds and warehouses. A few people in a liquor store, an Edward Hopper tableau, with their vans and pickups parked outside in from an empty road pointing inland into the fog void. They are, like most of us, natural libertarians generally unconcerned with things beyond their own diversion, their place on the land and with their families and friends, and their own profit and loss.

In the ocean just outside is the awareness of sounding whales from vast depths, of foreign ships with exterior languages and extrinsic food, all close by just beyond the power plant and liquor store.

Sea lions bark now and then past the wave break well out from the power plant's effluvial diffusing fans and feel the turbines' vibrations through their skin, muzzles and whiskers aquiver. They hold genetic memories of what has always been, as do the gray whales migrating past twice a year, Gulf of Alaska to calving lagoons in Baja California.

Ashore the yellow-lighted liquor store patrons, figures in caps glimpsed inside dirty Moss Landing windows, forget what's so close outside in the white-sauce thickening fog that's like a twilight of our time alive.

Generally only emptiness hangs at the sites of nature's ultimates. No heroics, no special label tags or qualities, just daily lives for those living there. And naturally there's rarely epic grandeur within individual lives no matter how grand their site may be. It's almost as though banality and significance coexist in like ratio, that expansiveness of soul comes as easily in standard, sheetrock, low-ceilinged rooms as to denizens of heroic natural sites.

Such amplitude is mostly gone in Moss Landing; at the end of the road in a cold California coastal fog manner. The flats beyond Castroville with the high-stack power plant sit there across the littoral of artichoke fields at the edge of the great and immense Pacific. While within the liquor store, sense of the ocean usually goes from the unacknowledged to the oblivious. Awareness gone like the substance of a northern Pacific foggy winter evening with not even a fog-horn's resonance or fish-splash focus for the depth of endless cold chill emptiness. Cold night fog in Moss Landing is that kind of being gone.

D. E. Steward

BLUE DEMONS

Dried many raindrops
Which fall down like blue demons
Died under tall corn crops
Stitch me an apron of ribbons

Steady now for more tomorrows
Days of worry
Ready to fall among shared sorrows
Ways of the crippled aged leopard

Eda Casciani

1sept03

that salty meat made you thirsty
luckily the water's still flowing
that kitchen tap is a marvel
can you imagine
what it'd be like if no water came out?
you could walk down
to the river or over to the supermarket
i understand it's nearly impossible to
filter out giardia
takes about as long to boil it as it does
to find out how to spell giardia in the dictionary
i'm not sure which is worse
giardia or coca cola

Mark Weber

AFTER THE DIAGNOSIS

For my husband

At breakfast you drink your coffee
as if it were medicinal tea, chew
your favorite cereal mechanically,
gaze at me with the mournful eyes
of a spaniel whose owner's suitcases
are packed and waiting by the door.

I say, Cheer up, Joe, It's not so bad.
And you sigh and laugh. I'm sorry,
Here I am acting so badly when
you're the one suffering from cancer.
Me, I'm only suffering from love.

Hilary Tham

CARE TO DANCE?

I walk in the dark
practicing for the day
when I'm not able to see.,
Funny how we remember
where we put our feet
just the other day
lights on or sun shining
how we step so sure
even before we fall.
In the dark I dance a bit slower
reach for your hand
with a smooth approach
wondering if I'll knock over
a lamp or hit the wall
on the way to our next waltz.

Tom Plante

AUTUMN ANGELS

The night nurses have placed
a carefully lettered sign
above the list of boarder babies,
the babies left behind
by their mothers,
bottle fed, wrapped, waiting,
names temporary,
unclaimed.

I hold one bundle,
all face,
sheets and blanket,
one hand on buttocks,
one hand on back of head.
We dance a moment
in the clerestory light:
open your eyes now,
Baby Boy Polite.

How often I too
have wanted
to walk away.

Turning the corner,
looking for home,
a single tree burns
red gold;
greets me
blesses me,

beauty in its death:
cold and loss,
color and light.

I pass.
Turn again.
I go
inside.

Kelly Jean White, MD

THE AZTEC TWELVE-STEP

i haven't had a drink in three weeks
and it hadn't seemed that big a deal

until i dreamed last night
that i was at a party town in mexico
and draining an endless array of
tequila and kahlua mixtures, tropical
rum concoctions, smooth irish coffees.

there were beautiful women there too,
attired as befit the climate,
and i was definitely aware of them,
they were not without interest to me –
one might say that i was sort
of working up to them.

but my main concern was
with the alcohol.
i had a lot of lost time
to make up for.

i was taking things
one night at a time.

Gerald Locklin

BATS IN THE BELFRY

If bats did not exist they would still end up coming through the window at nightfall. She saw the bats of her childhood swooping low over the manicured lawns.

She shuddered and resumed talking to her friend. But every once in a while would come unsummoned the bats of her childhood. Swiftly.

"You're flinching," her friend said. "What is it?"

"I hate manicured lawns."

"Tell me about it."

"I'm serious."

"What about them?"

"You'll think I'm crazy."

"I know that already."

"It's early evening, just starting to get dark –"

"Go on," her friend said.

"Time to come in," the parents are saying.

"And the children?"

"The children?"

"The children of the parents."

"The children are asking to stay out a little longer."

"And the bats?"

Patsy saw the bats of her childhood sweeping low over the manicured lawns. "There they are again," she whispered.

Sylvette put her arm around her friend. "I know, dear."

"I just feel like bawling."

"It's all right."

"I just feel like a basket case."

Sylvette slapped her friend upside the head. "Don't ever say that."

Patsy stared at her. She felt good. "Thanks."

Her friend smiled happily. She put her arm around Patsy's waist. "Yeah – what are friends for?"

They walked on together.

James Mechem

SOMETHING MIGHT HAPPEN

She's wearing a Tuesday mask
even though the calendar says Friday.
This is where math and poetry
break up, stop giving easy answers.
The value of truth becomes
fries and milk shakes.
Spring hats and snow
falling in the mountains. What's left
to trust? A man drinking a cold
beer trips over mid-afternoon.
She catches him in her arms
by the clock's midnight chime.
She's been looking for affection
all year. He's just been thirsty.
She steadies him into Wednesday
and lets go. The universe nods.

Ann Menebroker

sandwich

the old brown woman is stooped
like the ancient pines
that barely exist
up near the cold and windy timber line
she shuffles forward using the aluminum lawn chair
as ballast in front of her red tennis shoes
they are tattered
but laundered and darned
a large round black doily
crocheted especially for such occasions
drapes her head
a handsome usher wearing a wide rainbow ribbon
over his beefy shoulders
assists her in unfolding her chair
at the far right corner of the back of the room
she gratefully squeezes his hand so tightly
he winces
it's a good thing she has brought the chair
she knew the church would be crowded
the front page story covered half the page
about the deceased
and described a young man
stalwart in his efforts for social justice
she would not have been surprised
if the entire town had shown up for the service
whether they knew him or not
the service is already in progress
various friends are accounting
for his various acts of valor
in bravely facing forward
representing the disenfranchised
the overlooked
against the insensitive giants of government

how he used just plain common decency as his base
how he encouraged all to live freely in every aspect of their lives
          according to their own conscience
          (whatever that might dictate)
the old woman's swollen legs smolder like molten lead
          but if it were not for the balcony above her
          she believes she could raise up her arms
          and soar to the great sky
she wishes she had known the deceased
          and is pleased to have pasted the article
          in her scrapbook titled, *those who serve*
as a chorus of men assembles in the choir loft
          the old woman reaches into her rust knitted handbag
          and removes half a cold sandwich
          which she politely enjoys beneath her black doily
          as the men sing valiant songs
the songs cause the mourners to rise
          and feel proud to be alive
then the men close with, *somewhere over the rainbow*
the only dry eyes in the church
          are those of the old woman
          who remains calm and reverent
the ushers direct the crowd forward and past the altar
          which bears only an urn
          and numerous amusing photos of the deceased
the old brown woman once again reaches into her handbag
she removes the other half of the sandwich –
          neatly trimmed baloney and spicy mustard on white bread
she solemnly places it at the base of the urn

Spiel

6-16-04

Scattering ashes
in Florida nature

preserve at trailpoint
marker: “here today,

Gone tomorrow.”
Pausing to reflect,

scrub bluejays
perch nearby

expecting to be fed.

Alan Catlin

BAROMETER RISING

i’d come to take it
for granted that the day you turned fifty,
you began to feel awful,
and that each day
you felt a little worse.

now i still can’t quite believe
that, after fifty, improvement
is still possible.

Gerald Locklin

PREMARIN

Strange, magical, perhaps, taking
Premarin, that estrogen replacement
made from the urine of pregnant mares,
a strange kind of communion with the
Animal Kingdom, and, stranger, the
serendipity that enabled someone to
discover that a gestating mare could
bring civility, peace of mind and bones
to a woman no longer capable of birthing
anything but dreams and poems, but then
the Premarin began to make me ill and I
wondered if it was my mind over matter
or my fear of horses, as beautiful
as they are, something I'd rather behold
than ride, and so the doctor gave me
an estrogen patch made of something
he told me not to wonder about and today
when I threw away the old container
of Premarin, I wished it hadn't made me
ill, for I like the way wise ancients
wished upon the stars, the sun and moon to
claim kin with the animals and named
themselves Centaur, Issis, Tiger, La
Loba, Sitting Bull. I would've liked
naming myself Pinto, Palomino, or
Star-faced Mare Foaling Long-legged,
Eager-to-trot-and-suckle Colt.

Joan Jobe Smith

THE PRESCRIPTION

A poet in the pharmacy line is watching an old woman's liver-spotted hand
bounce to the countertop in time with the baton of the pharmacist's
directions. The old woman is hoping the handrhythm will work pnemonically,
her liver spots going like timpani mallets

TAKE 1 BLUE
PILL ON SUNDAY, THOSE ARE EQUAL TO 4 PINK PILLS, OKAY? THEN 1
OF THIS KIND IN THIS BOTTLE, TODAY, THERE ARE 3 OF THESE IN
THIS BOTTLE SO 1 BLUE PILL MON- I MEAN SUNDAY, REMEMBER 1
BLUE IS LIKE 4 PINK, SO YOU TAKE 1 OF THOSE AND YOU'LL HAVE
ENOUGH 'TIL WE CAN GET MORE

but the old
woman is lost, a hipwading fisher in a riptide of medi-syllables, the directions
pouring over her seawall brain, loose like live fish thumping in the
boatbottom of her
understanding

and a poet is no help standing there, staring at the pharmacist,
a thin thin woman with mascara *around* her eyes, halloweenish, skeletal, who
feels the implied criticism of the lengthening line and repeats herself, talking
slower, louder, so that the old woman, startles, self-conscious, pauses her hand
the way a frightened rabbit freezes, wishing to blend in with her surroundings,
embarrassed

customer eyes are flicking:
soldiers before battle tasting metal in their mouths *could the woman die if she*
forgets pink for blue?

and a poet is like a war photographer, soaking it in,
clicking the camera, detached, blandly alert, escaping to a memory of a
daughter who once became afraid like this, freezing like a liver-spotted old
rabbit on the peewee soccer field, camerahead staring helplessly at the
helpless daughter, clicking like a confused old woman's hand ticking time
before a death

and what good is a gawking poet and what good is a dying
old woman and what good is a poem about helplessness and what good is the
fragility of a good intention and what good is the outrageous distance
between any two people if no one ever finds a way to step out of the line
we're in, step out of line.

Frank Van Zant

CONSTANTIN BRANCUSI: *SLEEPING MUSE III*

i haven't had a muse for years.
women, yes, but not a muse, not since one
who made me feel first young, then old.
my children, yes, but it's not right to
lay too great a mythic burden on them:
let them grow on past your poems; free
them from your love of them.

graves needed his white goddess;
i don't.

perhaps the work, the medium, the
living are all one, and what we call
the muse is simply that we keep on doing
it. i think he put the muse to
sleep in his marble, or discovered that
she'd always slumbered there.

Gerald Locklin

THAT ELUSIVE CLARITY

once I bowled a 196,
as opposed to my usual 70 or 100.
I'm not lying.
For a short, shining moment
I *had* it,
I knew the game, had the skill,
knew what I had to do
to get there.

Then it was gone.

Poetry does that,
more often than not.

Michael Hathaway

I'VE NEVER WRITTEN A BASEBALL POEM

I didn't even make
the seventh grade
girls' third team

substitute.
Still can't
throw straight.

Last Easter, scrub game
with the kids,
I hit

a foul right through
Captain Kelly's French doors,
had to pay.

Still, these sultry
country nights
when I watch

the dark ballet
of players sliding
into base,

I shout "Safe!
He's safe! He's home!"
and so am I.

Elisavietta Ritchie

THE VALUE OF POETRY

A poem is a root, a tree, the sky, and a flower touched by the hands of a mystic. Poems are of value because life is of value. Often-times we speak the language of our fathers, for we share with them a sense of history. Down through history poetry has echoed man's hopes, his despair, his way of life and even the meaning of time to come ....

One must live and find life of value in order to write poetry. One must taste the essence of life, cope with tragedy, rise above disaster, and have a sense of that which is Infinite ....

I have labored for years to understand certain poems. Only now does their meaning loom clear. Only now does their significance reassure me. Knowledge becomes more pregnant as the seasons pass. The ultimate understanding of a difficult poem is the direct result of the passage of time. One grows as he ages, one has to stoop and be humble and know that comprehension can be as beautiful as love, as poignant as death, and as powerful as life itself.

Sue Abbott Boyd

the curse of poetry

is felt in the bones,
where it sticks like a cliché,
an overused word
that is somehow necessary
to hold the body and the text
together.

the promise of poetry
is in the collapse / of / the tower, /
and the angels singing
in the dust / rising
from chaos.

Joseph Farley

COMMENTARY

1

the difficulty
is
one likes things:
tactility
which bruises flesh
or iris or
tympanum.
what one responds
to
seems more than
his business
less than
his sum –
a slightness
of tongue.

2

still this makes
one's way
buckets of words
cranked up from
the well
their heaviness
weaving a bit
spilling symbols.
the dust buries
them quickly.
no matter.
most of the monads
are safe,
poured into
measured
transparencies ...

Hans Juergensen

This poem comes to you
like a pilgrim seeking shelter
from a storm
this poem makes its way
under the sheets
with no expectation
of favors or treats
this poem hovers in mid-air
like a hummingbird without
a care
this poem smells the aroma
of lavender soap
pressed to bath water skin
this poem needs no introduction
seeks no favors
comes in all flavors
this poem is a lover
a pilgrim a shaman
a voyeur camping inside
your heart
seeing through your eyes
this poem knows no restrictions
sets no conditions
this poem is strong as a steel dart
makes its nest inside your heart
this poem likes what it sees.

A.D. Winans

IN ALL THINGS GIVE THANKS

– St. Paul, I Thessalonians 5

"Eucharist," from the Greek
Eucharistia, Thanksgiving,
At each shared holy meal
We give thanks, even though
It is a celebration of death,
His death, it is a re-
Constitution of life,
His life, and a reminder
That we die and are alive
In Him and He is alive
In us, and we give
Thanks, not that we must die,
But that we live,
That we have the chance
To be alive under the sun,
That every precious anticipation
Suddenly turns to memory
Right before our eyes,
Like some little bird
Who comes to us if we feed it,
Who might hang around
Singing if it's satisfied
And then flies off
Whether we're ready
Or not.

Sander Zulauf

A SPACE FOR YOU TO KEEP A THOUGHT ON

CONTRIBUTORS

Duane Ackerson, of Salem, OR, is a long-time friend. Editor of *Dragonfly*, he was a major participant in the prose poem movement of the '70s. "Windows," p. 2, is from *Wounds Filled with Light*, Dragonfly Press, 1978; "In the Air," p. 45, was in *Caprice*; 2004; "Weathering," p. 58, is from *Weathering*, from *West Coast Poetry Review*, 1973.

Antler, the City of Milwaukee's widely-published Poet Laureate for 2002-3, has now had work in several KEP anthologies. "Childhood Visitation," p. 3 and "Save as an Idea," p. 17, are from his chapbook, *Exclamation Points ad Infinitum*, 2003, from Centennial Press, Milwaukee, WI.

Marie Asner of Overland Park, KS, is a busy woman at work in the fields of both music and writing. "Childhood Scenes," p. 14, is from her carefully researched and lovingly produced 2004 chapbook, *Amelia Earhart / Profile in Poems*. "The Passport," p. 51, came to us when we asked for poems.

Mel Belin is a fine photographer with an eye for both the seen and the invisible. Retired from the legal wrangles of Washington DC, he travels widely. He is the author of *Flesh that Was Chrysalis*, from Word Works' *Capital Collections*, 1999. "Dolphins and Sun Star," p. 27 and "Indian Summer in Atlantic City," p. 91, are previously unpublished.

Tom Bilicke edits the wonderful small journal, *Bosco: Helen's Dog Literary Review* in Los Angeles, CA. A friend to poets for many years, his own work appears infrequently. We are pleased to welcome "Biography," p. 35 which was previously unpublished, and "Smitten," p. 64, which first appeared in *Brevities* #14.

Dean Blehert's otherwise untitled poems, "Through sweat," p. 29 and "Icy rain," p.80 and "Lamplight, Your Hair," p. 106, are taken from Issue #110 of *Deanotations*, June 2004, which unfortunately was the final issue of that witty journal, produced at his home in Reston, VA. It will be missed.

Debra Bokur now lives in Nederland, CO, edits poetry for *Many Mountains Moving* and writes advertising for the Celestial Tea Company. Her gift of tea, with its lyrical box cover, prompted the "Nesting Boxes Poem" on p. 105; "St. Johns River, 1972," p. 38 and "April," p. 100, are new.

Sue Abbott Boyd headed South & West, Inc., an influential organization dedicated to furthering poetry nationwide, in Fort Smith, AK. "Time of Truth," p. 90, "A Time in Space," p. 61 and "Dinner on the Hotel Patio," p. 93, are from *How It Is*, from Olivant Press, 1968; "I Do Not...," p. 36 and "The Value of Poetry, p. 146, are from Vol. 14 #4, *South & West*, 1978.

Eda Casciani was the long-time editor and publisher of *Cardinal Poetry Journal*, from Cicero, IL. "Example" – an example of the Setto Bello form – p. 70 and "Blue Demons," p.133, a Scotch Braid, are republished from her chapbook, *Omnibus: Poems 1961-66*, from South & West, Inc., 1967.

Alan Catlin, Schenectady NY's most noted poet-bartender, recently hung up his slicers and bar rags for more time for his ever-expanding library of publications. "Reflections on the Masters," p. 48, "Two Scenes in the Manner of Turner," p. 122, and "6-16-04," p. 141, are new; "Island of the Oscillating Fans," p. 97, first appeared in *Edgz* # 8, 2004.

Grace Cavalieri, of Annapolis MD has authored fourteen books of poetry and twenty staged plays while also producing Public Radio's *The Poet & the Poem* for twenty-seven years. Mrs. P, the lively heroine of "The Light Has Feet," p. 59, makes frequent delightful appearances in Grace's work.

Tricia Cherin lives in Long Beach, CA, and has taught for many years in the English and Humanities and Interdisciplinary Studies departments at California State University's Dominguez Hills Campus. "Green Ban," p. 13, "Life Records," p. 36, and "Museum Work," p. 121, are previously unpublished.

David Chorlton was born in Austria but is now a resident of Phoenix, AZ. Author of KEP's latest single-poet volume – *A Normal Day Amazes Us*, 2003 – he was the featured poet at 2004's Poetry Rendezvous in Great Bend, KS. "Central Station," p. 92 is from *Lilliput* 1998; "Main Street," p. 130 and "Three Paintings in the Art Museum," p. 123, are new.

Robert Chute, a native of Maine, recently moved from Poland Springs to Brunswick, ME to be closer to his teaching work. He is a respected veteran of the small press as both poet and editor. "Parable of Three Deer Crossing a Field," p. 28 was first published in *Cafe Review*, 1991 and "This Machine Which Began," p. 31 is from *Epos*, 1973.

Peter Cooley lives in Jefferson LA, and teaches at Tulane University. "Meridian with Nocturne Subtext," p. 42 and "From Our Childhood," p. 126 are both from his book *A Place Made of Starlight*, 2003, from Carnegie Mellon University Press. "Rear View Mirror," p. 128, was in KEP's *Always the Beautiful Answer: a Prose Poem Primer.*

Silvia Curbelo was born in Matanzas Province, Cuba, where she lived until she was eleven. She now makes her home in Tampa, FL, where she works as an editor. "The Visitors," p. 37, first printed in *Crab Street Review*, is in her new book, *Ambush*, from *Main Street Rag*. "In the Locked Museum," p. 119, was first in *American Poetry Review.*

Bianca Diaz recently married a fellow poet. Originally from Miami, she took her MFA at George Mason University and now teaches sophomore English in Fairfax, VA. "The Ibis Finally Sends Back Her Interview Answers," p. 29 was first published in *So To Speak*, 2003. "Evolution of Wings," p. 53, is previously unpublished.

David Dunn (1953-1999) lived all his life in Brooklyn and New York City. "Poem," p. 96, was first published in *Pig Iron*. It will be reprinted again in the posthumous volume of his work, *The Lock of the Land*, edited by Ann E. Michael, and illustrated by Wayne Hogan. This long-awaited book from KEP should be in print by late fall of 2005.

John Elsberg, editor of *Bogg* and author of many collections, including *Off-sets* – an early KEP edition now in its 2nd printing – has called Arlington VA home for many years but is moving to the Maryland Eastern Shore. "The Green and Black Sedan," p. 129, is from *Offsets*, still available; "Auden on Yeats," p. 44, was in *Minotaur* #42, 2004.

Blair Ewing lives in Lutherville, MD, and like several other poets whose work is collected here, is active in the Bethesda-Washington DC area writers' scene, with frequent readings and appearances. "The Outer Rim," p. 20, was first published in the British journal, *Acumen.*

Joseph Farley is the publisher at Cynic Press in Philadelphia, PA. As such he has edited *The Axe Factory Review* for many years. "Drive," p. 128 and "the curse of poetry," p 146 are from his book *Suckers*, Cynic Press, 2004. Many of the poems in that collection appeared earlier in *Parnasus of World Poets 1999*, in Madras, India.

Maureen Tolman Flannery of Evanston IL, editor in 2000 of *Knowing Stones: Poems of Exotic Places* will soon publish a book of her own work, *Ancestors in the Landscape: Poems of a Rancher's Daughter*. Her poems "When the Stones Are Silent." p 46, "The Fisherman Is Old," p. 75, and "Thomas Tapes," p. 104, are previously unpublished.

Hugh Fox, known for his perspicacious reviews in *Small Press Review*, is another veteran poet and writer. He lives and writes in East Lansing, MI. "Eurydice," p. 60 is from his *The Face of Guy Lombardo*, a chapbook of prose poems from The Fault, in 1976. "A Major Evening Walk," p. 47, was written, I believe, for us.

Marvin Galvin of Chevy Chase, MD recently had the pleasure of reading his poetry at the Museum of Modern Art, responding to paintings in an exhibit picturing Old New England. His poem "Arts & Sciences," p. 9 appeared in *BigCityLit.com*, 2002. "Sun Dancers," p. 24 is previously unpublished.

Terry Godbey lives in Maitland, FL. Her poem "Alive," p. 15, took first place honors in the nearby Mount Dora 2004 Festival of Music and Literature, with publication in the *Mount Dora Topic*. Sadly, few people saw it there; hopefully, more may see it here. "Eight Years Old," p. 6 was first published in *Primavera* #27.

Lola Haskins of LaCrosse, FL teaches computer sciences at the University of Florida. "A Landscape With No People In It," p. 18 was in a 2004 *Caprice*; "Five Ways to Look at Blush," p. 117 was in a 2002 *Beloit Poetry Journal*; "Dearborn North Apartments," p. 66 and "Composition," p. 80 are from *Desire Lines*, BOA Editions, 2004.*

Jane Hathaway was the Assistant Editor for her son Michael's *Chiron Review*, and part of many wonderful humanitarian activities. She was surely the heart and soul behind the first Poetry Rendezvous, and she has attended every one since, in spirit. Her poem "Night," p. 16, is from *My Angel & Other Poems*, Chiron Review Press 1994.

Michael Hathaway was a teenager when he started editing *The Kindred Spirit*, which later became *Chiron Review*. He and his large family of cats live in the family home in St. John, KS, and he is the is the Curator of the Stafford County Historical Museum. "Birthright," p. 111 and "That Elusive Clarity," p. 144, are previously unpublished.

Wayne Hogan is the founding artist of KEP. Cartoonist, illustrator, poet and bon vivant teller of tales, he lives in Cookeville TN with his lovely wife, Susan. "The Sea," p. 21, "Epoxy," p. 30, and "The Whole Show, p. 71 are from *The Umbrella Poems*, a 2003 little books press collection with Joan Payne Kincaid. The cartoon beside "The Whole Show" was in a recent *Abbey*; and the "Jeweled Hatpins" poem p. 116 is also new.

Rochelle Lynn Holt, novelist, poet and teacher makes her home in Fort Myers, FL. She has several collections of verse from KEP, and has been part of our history from the start, as her Rose Shell Press printed the first Hogan-Kempher collaboration: *Mother Goose on Wheels*. "Rudimentary," p. 50 and "Gift of Parade," p. 63 are new for us.

Will Inman of Tucson, AZ was exchanging poems to this editor long before she was an editor, since they shared a common friendship with Evelyn Thorne, of *Epos*. Since then his work has graced several of the anthologies. The untitled poem, "I swim near ...", p. 23 was first in *Minotaur* #40; "song roots," p. 78 is from *Minotaur* #42, 2004.

Dorothy Jenks farms in Lakin, KS, where she has an active life with family and poetry. Her popular collection *Patterns of the Quilted Plains*, 1995, has been reprinted, and is still available. "Grandmothering," p. 8 is from that volume; "The Battle," p. 76 appeared first in *Friendly Creatures*, KEP 1995; "Four Mile Creek," p. 77 is new.

Frank Johnson, author of "Well Enough Alone," p. 102, sends poems from Tenants Harbor, ME, where he lives and writes by a tidal cove. His work has appeared in *Chiron Review* lately, and in over a hundred other periodicals."Well Enough Alone" is previously unpublished.

Colette Jonopulos, co-editor of the fine journal *Tiger's Eye*, lives in Eugene, OR where she tells us, Bob Marley and dreadlocks are still popular. She has two non-fiction books in print. "Then You Hear It," p. 41 and "Disruption in Primary Colors," p. 118 are previously unpublished.

Robert Joy of Great Bend, IN is a performance poet with several charming personnae, not the least of whom is Scarlett Sweetbriar, who once terrorized a guard at the Castillo de San Marcos. "Married to the Socks," p. 115, is from his 2002 collection, *Give Me an 'F'*, work selected by Karen Kline-Martin.

Hans Juergensen was born in Germany, but escaped to this country in 1934. While serving in the American Army, he was wounded at Anzio. Professor of Humanities at the University of South Florida in Tampa, he edited *Gryphon* for many years. "After Many Years," p. 61 and "Commentary," p. 147 are from *Florida Montage, South & West* 1966.

Marlene Kamei was once the proprietor and editor of Plumbers Ink Books, in Taos, NM. She was born in Kansas, but traveled extensively before settling in the southwest. *Stone Lantern Essays: services for the collapse of the living room carpet,* from which we took "Three Services," p. 40, was published by Plumbers Ink in 1980.

Ruth Moon Kempher established KEP in 1993 for the single purpose of publishing *The Prattsburgh Correspondence*, with Wayne Hogan's illustrations. Incredibly, *Unexpected Harvest* is our 28th publication. "Fields," p. 21 is from *Alphabit Soup*, little books press 1998. The poem with Debra Bokur, p.105, is new.

Joan Payne Kincaid, a multi-talented lady, lives in Sea Cliff, NY. A few copies of her book, *Understanding the Water*, 1997, are still available from KEP. "Do You Remember the Bluebirds? II," p. 35, was first in *Stray Dog*; 2004, "Chamber Music," p. 68, and "They Don't Serve Martinis ...," p. 86, are previously unpublished.

Herb Kitson, whose "Coffee House Improv" is on p. 70, teaches English and French at the University of Pittburgh at Titusville. His work has appeared in *Chiron Review*, and many other reviews, as well as in *To Life! Occasions of Praise*, from KEP, 2001. "Coffee House Improv" is previously unpublished.

Peter Klappert of Washington D.C. teaches in the graduate writing program at George Mason University. His former student, Bianca Diaz recommends him highly."Bright Moments Lakeside," p. 73, is from *Chokecherries: New and Selected Poems 1966-1999* from Orchises, 2000.

Mary Sue Koeppel, of Jacksonville FL, is the longtime editor of *Kalliope*, and author of *In the Library of Sciences, Poems of Loss*, from Rhiannon Press, 2001. Her second book of poetry, *With Desire* is scheduled for publication by Canopic Press, and will include "Andante Love," p. 93 and "Where We Lay and Made Snow Angels," p. 99.

Steve Kowit, a Brooklyn native who now calls California home, teaches at Southwestern College in Chula Vista. He is the author of several chapbooks, including *The Dumbbell Nebula*, Roundhouse 2000, and editor of *The Maverick Poets*, an anthology. "Kiss," p 98 and "Snapshot," p. 34 are new.

Peter Krok of Havertown, PA is the editor of the *Schuykill Valley Journal*, and has coordinated a poetry series at the Manayunk Art Center since 1990. His poetry has appeared in numerous journals, including *Ruah*, which first published "Names of Things," p.43.

Kyle Laws, originally from the New Jersey coast, now lives in Pueblo, CO, where she has an accounting and financial advisory company. She co-authored, with Tony Moffeit, a KEP 1997 popular edition, *Tango*."Stranded," p. 103 is previously unpublished; "Debris," p. 95 was first printed in *Chiron Review*.

Lyn Lifshin, now from Vienna VA, has published more than one hundred volumes of poetry, edited four anthologies of women's writing, and had innumerable single poems in assorted journals. "White Trees in the Distance," p. 32, "My Neighbor in Her Veils," p. 49, and "From the Porch in Almost Darkness," p. 82, were previously unpublished.

Gerald Locklin teaches in Long Beach, CA. He has authored numerous collections, including the now out of print *The Hospital Poems* from KEP 1998, from which "The Aztec Twelve Step," p. 136 and "Barometer Rising," p. 141 were taken. "Constantin Brancusi: Sleeping Muse III," p.144 is from *running into ger*, Royal Vagrant, 1999.

Virginia Love Long lives on land in Hurdle Mills, NC which has been in her mother's family for five generations. Her chapbook *Squaw Winter* was *Kindred Sprit/Chiron Review's* first chapbook. It won the Oscar Arnold Young Book Award (Poetry Council of NC) in 1988. She has had several from that press since then. "Prairie Song," p.77, celebrating Kansas, is new, for us all.

James Mechem edits *Caprice* from New York City, after years of *Out of Sight* from Wichita. Now retired from the reading spotlight, he was once an extremely hard act to follow. "All that Glitters, Shirley," p. 67, and "Bats in the Belfry," p. 137, were first published in *Caprice*.

Ann Menebroker edited the lively little journal, *Impulse*. She lives in Sacramento, CA, having downsized from a house to an apartment. There are probably poems in that move. "Pulling the Caution Light," p. 4 was first in *The Tule Review*, 2003, and "Something Might Happen," p. 138, was a broadside from Bottle of Smoke Press, 2004.

Ann E. Michael of Emmaus, PA is the chief editor of David Dunn's collection, due from KEP in the near future. Her own poetry has appeared in several of our collections. "Tangles," p. 5 was first published in *Minimus*; "*Wu Wang*: Innocence," p. 72 first appeared in *Studia Mystica.* A second I Ching Poem, "*T'ai*: Peace," appears on p.79.

Tony Moffeit has traveled from Pueblo, CO to be the headline, featured performer at many a Poetry Rendezvous, starting with Great Bend, and St. John, Kansas, and gracing Savannah GA and St. Augustine, FL gatherings too. Co-author, with Kyle Laws, of KEP's *Tango*, he has many collections to his credit. "Coyote's Sermon ...," p. 89, is new.

Miles David Moore of Alexandria VA, hosts the popular Iota Reading Series at a murky pub in nearby Arlington, and is an active editor on the Word Works Press staff in Washington, DC. "'I Love Barbie Taylor. T. Mc.,'" p. 101, is taken from his book, *The Bears of Paris*, from Word Works' Capital Collection, 1995.

Sheila Murphy, a Phoenix, AZ Instructor of English, deserves many thanks for her support of our various projects, especially those involving prose poetry. Her prose poem "Maybe romance dampens," p. 65, was in *Leaflets*, from Instress, 1998; "Miami," p. 92 in *Abbey* #70, 1993. "Brushstrokes at Daybreak ..." p. 107 was a recent New Year's greeting.

Robert Novak spent many years teaching at the Purdue-University of Indiana extension in Fort Wayne, IN, where he edited *The Windless Orchard.* He has lately retired from those two jobs, but still lives in Fort Wayne. "Thinking It Over," p. 110, is from his chapbook, *The Hemingway Poems*, Windless Orchard Press, still available.

Maureen Owen edited the eclectic journal *Telephone* for many years. Her poem "What do you do when you can't forget the one you / don't love anymore," p. 56, was originally published in *Untapped Maps*, from Potes & Poets Press, 1993, and was later a part of KEP's celebrated prose poem primer, *Always the Beautiful Answer*.

Tom Plante continues to produce and edit *Exit 13* – an almost annual publication that since 1988 has featured poetry of people, places and travel – from his home in Fanwood, NJ. He also works for Union County's department of public information. His poems "Care to Dance?" p. 134 and "The Plan for Today," p. 108 are new to us.

Jeff Poniewaz lives in Milwaukee, WI where he teaches Literature of Ecological Vision at UW-M. His last name, pronounced "Poe-nyeah-vahsh," is Polish for "Because." His two poems, "Ocean Reunion," p. 19 and "Watering the Garden," p. 87 are from his book *Dolphin Leaping in the Milky Way*, from Inland Ocean Books, 1986.

Elisivietta Ritchie of Broomes Island, MD has many fine books to her credit. "Root Soup, Easter Sunday," p 52, is from *Flying Time: Stories and Half Stories*, Signal Books, 1996; "Like Eve ...," p 83, from *Awaiting Permission to Land*, due in 2005, "I've Never Written a Baseball Poem," p. 145 is from *The Arc of the Storm*, Signal Books 1998.

Linda Rocheleau of Savannah, GA hosted Poetry Rendezvous 2003 in her lovely city. As well as writing poetry and conducting workshops, she works as a writer of grants for her School Board. Her poem "The Perfect Crime," p. 85, was first published in *Chiron Review*. "Most Matters Can Be Ironed Out," p. 114, is new.

Margaret Shauers lives in Great Bend, KS, where she is an active worker with whatever writers' groups are ongoing: she has been involved with the Poetry Rendezvous happenings from the start. "Become as a Child," p. 8, was first published in the Advent booklet of the First Presbyterian Church of Great Bend.

Shivaree is the working name of a longtime friend of KEP. Her poems, illustrations and short prose have graced several of our anthologies. After spending her youth in the Midwest, she now makes her home in Sandwich, MA. Her vignette "Out There," p. 57, is a new work.

Joan Jobe Smith, who is a founding co-editor of the estimable journal *Pearl*, lives in Long Beach, CA with her poet husband, Fred Voss. Her poems "Love Beads," p. 113, and "Premarin," p. 142, are from *a spy in a broccoli forest*, which was the chapbook contest winner from *Sheila-Na-Gig* in 1997.

Carolyn Sobel is a Professor of Linguistics at Hofstra University, living in nearby Rockville Centre, NY. Her poems "Little Brother," p. 7 and "Playscript," p. 69 are from an her book *Intermissions*, an early best-seller from KEP in 1995, with illustrations by Margo Hammond. Only a few copies of this fine book are still available.

Laurel Speer, once the writer of opinion for *The Small Press Review*, and always a fine poet, lives in Tucson, AZ. "On the Occasion of My Daughter's 40th Birthday," p. 10 is new to us, but "Platte River Girl." p.75 and "My White Buck Shoes," p. 112 are from the chapbook, *Platte River Girl.*

Spiel, of Pueblo West, CO calls himself "white, old, and a maverick." His poems "revelation," p. 64 and "unseen guest," p. 82 appeared in a recent *Abbey*; "sandwich" p. 139 was first published by Pudding House, in *Human*, 2003. "deceit," p. 109 has been in *Free Verse* and *Slipstream.* "green night," p. 22 is new for us.

D. E. Steward, of Princeton NJ, has had work published in the small press for many years. His bird and other wildlife poems, sometimes illustrated, have graced several KEP editions, including *Joyful Noise (Friendly Creatures #2)* in 1996 from which "Reeds Gap," p. 125 was taken. "Moss Landing, California," 130-132 is new for us.

Dan Stryk lives in Bristol, VA and teaches literature and creative writing at Virginia Intermont College there. He is the author of five collections of poetry and creative non-fiction, including *Taping Images to Walls, informal sonnets* from Pecan Grove Press. "The Ironweed that Will Not Fade," p. 25 and "In the British Museum," p. 120, are new.

William E. Taylor retired from the English Department of Stetson University, to his home in New Smyrna Beach, FL. During his active years, he edited several journals, including *Poetry Florida, &*, and was poetry editor of *Florida Education*. "Ideals," p. 16 and "Old Records," p. 115 are from *Down Here with Aphrodite*, South & West Inc., 1966.

Hilary Tham, born in Malaya, but now of Arlington VA, is editor-in-chief of Word Works. "The Naming," p. 39 and "Mrs. Wei in America," p. 55 are from *Bad Names for Women*, a Word Works Capital Collection, 1989; "Toll Road," p. 127 is from *Reality Check* – her travel poems and art from KEP in 2001. "After the Diagnosis," p.134 is new.

Evelyn Thorne with her husband Will Tullos, for many years hand-produced *Epos*, a fine journal.from Crescent City, FL. She continued producing *Epos* for some time after his death. "Have You Seen Her," p. 12 and "Flute," 81 are from *Ways of Listening*, her book from Olivant Press, 1969.

Frank Van Zant whose 2000 KEP book of baseball poetry, *The Lives of the Two-Headed Baseball Siren* is now sold out, coaches other people's kids as well as his own, and is a teacher and advisor to hard-to-handle youth in Long Island's East Northport, NY area."How the Thing Lateisha Says ..." p. 11 and "The Prescription," p. 143, are new.

Fanny Ventadour spent her childhood in New Orleans, then lived in Paris for many years, staying in France through the Occupation. Finally, she was a resident of Winter Park, FL. "Jonquils Can Happen," p. 72 is from *The Centre Holds*, 1977 Editions Two Cities, who also had published "Too Late the Heliotrope," p. 86, in *Blue Is Recessive as in Irises* in 1966.

Chick Wallace now of Gainesville, FL is the heroine of a real-life romance as she will soon marry a gentleman whom she had not seen for many years, until they recently met again after both had married others, raised families, and lost their mates. Her poem "The Beanpicker's Daughter Learns to Read," p. 54 is previously unpublished

Susan Weaver, the author of the previously unpublished "Triptych: Celebrating April," p. 74 lives in Allentown, PA, where she works as a freelance journalist, editor and poet. Her cycling articles have appeared in a wide variety of magazines, and she authored the book, *A Woman's Guide to Cycling*, from Ten Speed Press, 1998.

Mark Weber owns and operates Zerx Press and Zerx Records in Albuquerque, NM, "(Borges, non-fiction, selected)" p. 33 appeared in *Minotaur*, but is also collected in *Optimism ads Skepticism*, Zerx Press, 2003, from which "4sept03 [i just vacuumed]" p. 84 and "1sept03 [that salty meat]" p. 133 were also taken.

Kelley Jean White, M.D. has been an inner-city pediatrician with a practice in Philadelphia, PA for more than twenty years. "Eight Months," p. 10 and "Autumn Angels," p. 135 were published in her book *The Patient Presents*, from The People's Press, 2001.

Jill Williams divides her time between Vancouver, British Columbia, and Sedona, AZ. Author of the 1974 Broadway musical *Rainbow Jones*, she travels widely, giving much-acclaimed performances of her work. "Nitobe Garden," p. 94 was first published in *A Weakness for Men*, Woodley & Watts, Inc. 2003.

A. D. Winans still lives in his native San Francisco, where for years he edited the Beat journal, *Second Coming*, a period of his life chronicled in *Charles Bukowski: The Second Coming Years*, from the Beat Scene Press, 1996. "Untitled" p. 62 and the really untitled poem beginning "this poem comes ...," p.148, are new for us.

Thalia Xynides, the author of the previously unpublished "Virtuosi," p.71 made her first anthology appearance in the earlier KEP collection, *To Life! Occasions of Praise*, 2001. She is closely associated with the owner of the Press, who can vouch for the fact that this poem was written specifically for this volume.

Sander Zulauf lives in Andover, NJ and edits the prestigious *Journal of New Jersey Poets* from the County College of Morris, in Randolph NJ. "Always Less," p. 88 was originally published in *Blueline*, Vol XIV, and "In All Things Give Thanks," p.149 first appeared in *5 AM*, Issue 18.
